BLUEY WILKINSON

WEST HAM'S FIRST WORLD CHAMPION

BLUEY WILKINSON

WEST HAM'S FIRST WORLD CHAMPION

Brian Belton

Foreword by Tony Durant

TEMPUS

Frontispiece: Wilkinson triumphant!

First published 2004

Tempus Publishing Ltd
The Mill, Brimscombe Port
Stroud, Gloucestershire GL5 2QG
www.tempus-publishing.com

British Library Cataloguing in Publication Data.
A catalogue record for this book is available from the British Library.

ISBN 0 7524 2872 1

Typesetting and origination by Tempus Publishing
Printed and bound in Great Britain

CONTENTS

The Duchess of Kent congratulates Bluey Wilkinson as she presents him with the trophy at a Special Challenge Match in 1939.

ACKNOWLEDGEMENTS

This book owes a tremendous debt to Allen Trump. Allen is not only a dedicated fan of speedway; he is one of the very few diligent custodians of its history. Not an expert, one who only knows speedway, but an intellectual of the sport, someone who brings intelligence and solid values to his passion. Without the likes of Allen, the sport of speedway would have lost its past and as such have no future. Allen, by his generosity, care and effort, has given a great gift to this book's audience and as such future generations that might derive meaning, purpose or just plain enjoyment from speedway.

I would also like to thank Sid Stanley, a fellow West Ham supporter of the 1960s and 1970s, who has also made a big contribution to this work by his patience and munificence. Reg Fearman, former West Ham rider, England manager and promoter, has been good enough to read through these pages and correct errors of fact and history. Tony Durant was kind enough to undertake the introduction while making a video record of Bluey's life. Tony's father Don used to race against Bluey during Wilkinson's first years in Britain. Tony still has the West Ham Championship Trophy that his dad left to him. Don had won it in 1932 riding against Bluey. In true Custom House traditions the race was quite novel. Both bikes continually shed their chains after the first two laps of the contest. Don and Bluey were good friends and Tony has told me that Bluey's name was often referred to in the Durant household as 'a shining example of the perfect Australian gentleman… unlike the rest of 'em!'

Finally there is my son's mother, Rosy, who has laboured through my words with a critical eye that has not always been merciful. She is an Irish/Flemish/north London diamond and still the best teacher I have ever known. Our boy Christian has always been there, making me see what truly matters in our existence; the experience of being together. This is the spirit that I hope will come through in this story of Bluey Wilkinson, 'The Custom House Comet' and the 'Bathurst Flyer', how he brought people together and that he, his era and those who defined those times, the fans and the riders, might come together with you.

Thank you.

Brian Belton

FOREWORD

Bluey Wilkinson was a name I was brought up with. My father Don Durant raced alongside Bluey in the pioneer days at West Ham in 1929. Over Sunday lunch, Bluey's name was often brought up in conversation as a shining example of chivalry, keen sportsmanship and sheer guts. The West Ham Championship Trophy graced our mantelpiece. My father was, in his own words, 'a quite unworthy winner' against such a great rider. He was, as my father would pronounce in his powerful English public school voice, 'An absolute gentleman, quite unlike the rest of that Aussie rabble!' But as a child back then, to me he was little more than just a name.

Thirty years later, living in Australia, I was lucky enough to meet and become great friends with Muriel, Bluey's wife and sweetheart from those 'golden years'. She produced a photo which I had never seen, taken on the start line at West Ham; two fresh faced boys, a seventeen and a twenty-year-old, Bluey and my father, lined up with legends like Tiger Stevenson. As my friendship with Muriel grew, I came to learn with affection something about the man who had been little more than a name from my childhood.

Muriel would have loved this book. It recreates Bluey's childhood in Bathurst, NSW, Australia. While it chronicles Bluey's outstanding career, it gives a revealing insight into that extraordinary period when speedway threatened to sweep all before it to rival soccer as England's number one sport. We are there in the East end of London, experiencing the sheer excitement on the terraces at West Ham in the 1930s, as Bluey, Jack Parker, Sprouts Elder and the great Vic Huxley created their magic. Brian has dug deep in his research and personal stories from eye witnesses give great colour and character to the book. We come to know something of the men who raced alongside Bluey and the many battles he fought, as we follow Bluey's determined struggle to achieve his goal and reach speedway immortality. As such, the book becomes a chronicle for the speedway historian. It not only follows the career of the 'Bathurst Flyer', as he was affectionately known, but provides a rich backdrop to the man in his

Opposite: 'Andsome Arthur Atkinson.

Above left: Alec Statham.

Above right: Tiger Stevenson.

time. It is illuminating that in the midst of the 'do or die' encounters he faced almost daily, he never let malice cloud his judgement. He was referred to as 'the Sphinx'. No one seemed to have had a bad word to say about Bluey. His legendary status was confirmed when he was invited out of retirement for one last race before royalty in which he convincingly beat England's best, Arthur Atkinson.

Bluey did everything right. He won the World Championship in 1938, then retired at the summit of his achievements to enjoy life as a family man. With his untimely death, Muriel lost her one true soulmate and the sports world lost a great ambassador. His death remains one of life's great tragedies.

I'm sure you will enjoy Brian's book as I did.

Tony Durant

INTRODUCTION

This book celebrates one of Australia's greatest ever motor-sport heroes, Arthur George Wilkinson, the Bathurst Flyer, Bluey Wilkinson. However, his sporting home in the Docklands of East London, was, perhaps particularly in his heyday, the 1930s, about as far as one might get from the place of his birth. It was one of the poorest and most working class areas in the United Kingdom, a hotbed of industry and industrial politics. The people who supported West Ham Speedway, the team Bluey rode for throughout his rise to fame and eventual triumph, placed loyalty and character above all else in terms of human qualities and it was probably this that endeared Wilkinson to them and them to Bluey. He became one of their own, not just for the ten or so years he rode for the Hammers but forever, as evidenced by a poll undertaken by *Speedway '72* magazine, just after West Ham speedway had fallen silent forever, which looked to identify West Ham's greatest ever rider. Bluey Wilkinson tied with his fellow Australian and West Ham's second World Champion Jack Young in the vote. However Jack's exploits were still fresh in the memories of many fans and it says quite something for the 'Boy from Bathurst' that he was still well remembered over thirty-three years after his tragic, untimely death.

Bluey has a statistical record second to none, and there are many fine publications that have recorded the facts and figures relating to his achievements in comparison to his peers and rivals (for example Peter Jackson's *Speedway Archives*). As such, I have not attempted to merely replicate such material. While I do not agree with a friend of mine who sees such data as the product and province of the 'speedway anorak', I do feel that those of us with a passion for the sport as it once was do risk getting somewhat weighed down by such material. As the piles of statistics grow they tend to threaten to obscure the facet of the speedway that gave it a mass appeal; the men (and the few women), the human beings, with personalities, desires, ambitions, qualities and flaws who populated and contested the speedways of Britain and the world. This is why I have chosen to look, as much as possible, at Bluey Wilkinson the dedicated rider but also at the person under the leathers, a man with a good heart and a fine soul.

Having taken this task on, I found that Bluey is very much a legend. What was written about him in the newspapers and the speedway press during and after his track career

Opposite: West Ham before the
Hammers (note the halved tabards and
the very young Bluey, third from right).

Left: Hammers one and two.

Below: Jack Young with Frances Day –
they didn't win the heat.

is either entirely factual information about his performances, sometimes not totally accurate, or strange 'wowee' stories that elaborate, embroider and/or exaggerate events. You have only to read the first few pages of the book written by his associate, friend, compatriot and manager at West Ham Johnnie Hoskins, *Bluey Wilkinson, World Champion*, to see the style. It portrays Wilkinson as an odd mixture. At some points he is depicted as a happy-go-lucky Brian Rix-type 'chap', whose life is a sort of speedway version of an Ealing comedy, involved in all sorts of 'scraps' and 'jolly japes'. A turn of a page gives a picture of our hero as an Aussie John Wayne, swashbuckling around Britain, alternating between a hard, driven, 'lone rider' and a 'man's man', in with a group of fellow racers, loveable rogues all. You can almost hear the frenetic knee and back-slapping fest. It seems that even before his death, Bluey was something of a legend; now his life has become the stuff of myth. In more ways than one he was, as he was called, the 'Bathurst Blur'.

So when I started this project some years ago, I went to New South Wales just to get an idea of the kind of place where Arthur Wilkinson was born and brought up. I think I learnt more about him just being there and back at home in the East End of London than anywhere else. I talked to people about him and from there reading the literature and picking out the wheat from the chaff seemed to get easier. For example, my great-uncle, just before he passed away in the spring of 2002, told me that around the track where Bluey made his name he was known as 'The Custom House Comet'. I had heard this before, from stories told to me by my grandfather who worked at Custom House Stadium, but the information had slipped away with my childhood days. This was the man I was looking for! I found Bluey, a relatively straightforward man, a human of his place and time, wrought out of and helping to produce his context but like all heroes and champions, he was an ordinary person with something exceptional.

Left: Johnnie Hoskins finds the Holy Grail.

Opposite: Young Bluey practising.

The Name, the Man

Bluey Wilkinson is a name that anyone associated with the world of speedway will know. Ivan Mauger, another World Champion and speedway immortal, who also promoted speedway in Bathurst, Bluey's home town, once commented that Australia's cricketers are celebrated and admired in a number of nations. However, the champions of speedway are noted and commemorated by many millions right across the face of the globe and wherever speedway is organised and watched, Bluey Wilkinson of Bathurst is remembered. He was a favourite with the millions of supporters who followed the sport throughout the 1930s and a hero to those who followed after him.

The youth of contemporary Antipodean speedway know of Bluey and when they follow the path he trod to Britain they find that his name and achievements are still savoured by those who lived the sport as competitors or spectators. To this extent Wilkinson is a strong link in the sporting bridge that connects Australia to the rest of the world and especially the area of London where I was born and brought up to respect his memory. For all this, Bluey Wilkinson was a quiet, modest and unassuming person. Keeping himself to himself he was something of a loner. Few had any idea of what he was thinking or how he thought. Perhaps that's why he was also known as 'the Sphinx'. At the same time he did have the determination, ambition, drive, resolve and courage to become champion in what was, in his era, one of the world's toughest and most exacting sporting realms.

1

MILLTHORPE, BATHURST, CUSTOM HOUSE

Arthur George Wilkinson was born in the small and elegant rural town of Millthorpe on 27 August 1911. Millthorpe was no more than a village when Arthur, or Bluey as he was to become nicknamed and universally known because of his red hair and freckles, first saw the light of day.

In close to 100 years since Bluey's birth, Millthorpe has grown in heritage importance as an outstanding example of an Australian country town of the late nineteenth/early twentieth century, with historic and aesthetic qualities. When researching this book I visited Millthorpe. It boasted a number of stylish cafés and galleries and had the feel of latter-day elegance. It is not far from the town of Blayney but the nearest city of any size is Bathurst which lies just east of Millthorpe. At the age of four, Bluey and his family moved to Bathurst, to a small weatherboard cottage in Violet Street South. In 1916 Bathurst was the type of place where everybody knew everybody and the Wilkinson family soon became part of the place and considered it their home.

The City of the Plains

Sometimes referred to as the 'City of the Plains', Bathurst is Australia's oldest inland settlement (and city). It is around 200km west of Sydney and it took me around two and a half hours to drive there from that impressive harbour city.

Bathurst played an essential part in the settling of Australia. When the coastal plains around Sydney reached their limit in terms of grazing capacity, George Evans and a party of explorers pushed a trail across the Great Dividing Range and found the rolling lush countryside on the western slopes of the mountains. This might well be thought of as the point at which Australia's future was sealed.

Very quickly cattle, sheep and crop farming were established and these activities swiftly developed. Bathurst was proclaimed a town in 1815 and, with the discovery of gold, experienced rapid growth throughout the mid-nineteenth century. It was gazetted as a city in 1885. As such, Bathurst has some superb examples of colonial architecture with an abundance of heritage buildings. The main streets are a delightful mixture of old and new, with charming cast-iron Victorian lamp-posts adorning busy shopping centres. The Sir

Joseph Banks Nature Reserve is also a real feature, capturing the outback roots of the city, with its koalas, kangaroos and wallabies in huge and picturesque parklands.

The beautiful courthouse, which luxuriates in Victorian Renaissance style, is the home to the Bathurst Historical Museum and captures the spirit of Bathurst, as does the nearby Boer War memorial. The latter bears the name of Lieutenant Peter Handcock, who was shot along with Harry 'The Breaker' Morant for murdering Boer prisoners. This episode of Australian colonial history became a successful film staring Edward Woodward.

In the days of the gold rush, Bathurst was the nearest town to the goldfields of Ophir, Sofala, Rockley and O'Connell. If ever you go to Bathurst you can hire panning equipment and try your hand at finding the yellow treasure. I hope you have more luck than I did! But I did come across a certain type of fortune.

Of Boys and Men

Sitting outside a quaint restaurant I began talking to a man who introduced himself to me as Bob Ratchet. Bob told me that his father, Rob, had raced Bluey Wilkinson on the Bathurst speedway back in the 1920s. The elder Ratchet had been something of a local champion, riding against other men for fun and wagers on a machine he was constantly adapting and adding to, so much so that it was hard to call it by a maker's name, it being such a hybrid. Bob told me how his dad had accepted a head-to-head challenge from Bluey, having beaten the young man in a six-man race some weeks before.

The two-header had been a dour contest, a battle of bends rather than a race on straights. Going into the last turn the lad, no more than sixteen at the time, although riding a heavier bike, was, partly because of his lighter body weight, leading. To avoid humiliation the older rider cut into the bend, making the most of his greater strength, body mass and utilising the superior muscle of his machine to take the inside. Wilkinson though was not about to give up his ground without a fight and pushed his rival tight, forcing Rob to sink low in his saddle and lift his leg to hold on to velocity. Bob became quite animated, miming the actions of a track racer of old. He told of how his father had recalled a near-panic moment as he felt his bike wobble between equilibrium and disaster, staggering along the border of stasis and chaos but Rob had hung on, calling in all his chips of luck and knowledge in the process to hold his line and the advantage. The extra horsepower at his command took him home and Bluey was again beaten, but only just: the thickness of a tyre had separated the experienced rider from the teenager.

Bluey had emptied his pockets to pay the victorious Ratchet but such was the man's admiration for the boy that he had told young Arthur to hold on to his money, advising the little redhead to put it towards a better machine, for if they had matched each other mechanically Arthur Wilkinson would have taken the day. The practised scratch rider had to concede that the ginger lad, whose legs were hardly able to reach the ground once aboard his bike, was much more a racer than he. Rob, although he went on to appear with his brother Todd in 'Wall of Death' shows around New South Wales (my correspondent Bob joined the troop for a few years), was never to ride in competition again, but Bluey was to go on to rule the world.

I heard a similar story some months later. This time the teller was a woman who was in front of me in a post office queue in Canning Town. The 'dark rider' was her grandfather, Charlie Charles, and Bluey had won the day. It seems that if you scratch the surface in New South Wales or E16 quite a few people might well have a tale to tell about Mrs Wilkinson's lad. Few, maybe none would be untruths, but all are testament to a man who in his few short years hammering round this earth, became a jouster of mythical proportions; a legend of speed.

A Heritage of Speed

When Bluey Wilkinson was a boy, food and timber processing, railway locomotives and transport dominated the Bathurst economy. Although these manufacturing industries have not disappeared, Bathurst is now more a university city than anything else; one of the largest employers in the city is Charles Stuart University. Other concerns include numerous public and private high schools, the Conservatorium of Music, the Surveyor General's Department and the Correctional Centre which also provide employment opportunities. However, the city of Bathurst has a heritage of speed. Motorcycle racing is generally believed to have started in Bathurst in 1911, the year of Bluey Wilkinson's birth, on the roads around the area at the edge of the city known as Mount Panorama. Speedway commenced in 1931 on the Vale Circuit. This continued until 1937, when the circuit at Mount Panorama was completed. The first race was held there in March 1938. Mount Panorama has hosted various Australian Grand Prix, for both motorcycles and open four-wheelers. Since October 1963 the city has become both the spiritual and physical home of touring-car racing in Australia and today Bathurst is, for most Australians, virtually synonymous with motor racing. Bathurst is known throughout the world as the host city of an annual road race on Mount Panorama. Each year the 6.213km of public road around Panorama transforms into the world-renowned Mount Panorama racing circuit and becomes the focus for over one billion people worldwide. It is the premier racing circuit in Australia, Mount Panorama being the only permanent public road-racing circuit on that continent.

The city's association with motor sport is also confirmed by it being the home of the National Motor Racing Museum (NMRM) which is a unique Australian attraction located beside the motor-racing circuit but, of course, it will always be the home of World Speedway Champion, Bluey Wilkinson. As such he was a product and part of the root of Australia's unique motor-sport tradition.

Demon of the Courts, Heart of the Family

The Wilkinson home in Violet Street had a tennis court beside it and the family were keen players. Bluey always enjoyed the game. However, his manager at West Ham, Johnnie Hoskins, was also a keen player and would often claim that he might not have been able to better Bluey on the track but had the ability to humble him on the court. In defence, Bluey always countered that he could beat Johnnie Hoskins barefoot. When the game finally took place both contestants shunned footwear and it was the Wilkinson feet that took the laurels. Post-match, Hoskins commented that if Bluey had not become World Champion in speedway he would have become a champion tennis player. The rider played tennis like he rode. He chased every ball and he used his intellect to overcome his opponents. Like many other world speedway champions he could probably have become a champion in other sports but the sport which captured his heart, mind and soul from the very beginning was speedway.

Later, Bluey and his family moved to Piper Street, where they lived when Bluey started racing. His brothers Bob, who was to visit Bluey during his time in Britain, and Eric, liked to ride motorbikes but never entertained any plans to follow their famous brother. Bluey's sister Jean was always very proud of him. Although he was to become world famous, Bluey Wilkinson remained a quiet, private person who loved his family and his home town. Throughout the 1930s, which turned out to be the last decade of his life, whenever he returned to Australia for three months of the year, he spent as much time as possible with his family in the 'Queen City of the Plains'.

The Racer is Born

Bluey's dad was a butcher in Bathurst. As a boy young Arthur would peddle furiously, seemingly putting himself and the rest of the town's populace at risk, delivering meat. Speedway was a sport in the throes of its earliest development in 1928 when, on the evening of 29 September, Bluey went to see his first and the Bathurst's initial official dirt-track meeting. New South Wales was one of the hotbeds of the young sport of speedway at that time and Bluey was as taken with it as most other young men in the state were. Arthur was barely sixteen years old, a freckle-faced red-headed boy who worked as a butcher's delivery boy and did a bit of work around a local garage. He made his way to the meeting on the pushbike he used to undertake his rounds. The young Wilkinson had already earned a local reputation as a bit of a daredevil on an ordinary pushbike. He could slide his back wheel round corners and would often race between pedestrians, leaving them untouched but shocked by the whirlwind that had encompassed them. As such it is perhaps unsurprising that Bluey became immediately captivated by what he saw at his first sight of organized speedway. His eye for detail that was to stand him in such good stead in the future, took in the nuances, foibles and demeanour of the riders he watched, how their machines responded, twisted, turned, sped and slowed. He deciphered the tactics and strategy used in the fights for position that dominated the struggles for victory. Completely mesmerised, he wandered undetected into the riders' enclosure. Maybe his look or enthrallment camouflaged him, made him look like he belonged? The lad overcame his natural shyness, talking to and questioning the leather-clad warriors as they tended the monsters they had ridden or were about to ride. At the end of that Saturday night Bluey had decided that his future would be bound within the ovals of dreams that were the speedways of the world.

Although it would be three more years before speedway became established in Bathurst, *The Times of Bathurst* reported the city's initial introduction to the sport with some enthusiasm on the morning of Monday 1 October 1928:

> *In the presence of a large crowd of spectators, including visitors from many distant parts, the Bathurst Speedway was officially opened on Saturday night, and had a most successful and gratifying inauguration.*

A very large programme of events was contested and produced several thrilling finishes. As was to be expected in this exciting and daring sport, the night was not without its spills as well as thrills and several riders crashed, fortunately with only one serious injury. The official opening was performed by the Mayor of Bathurst (Alderman J.A. Hitchcock). He concluded:

In the matter of sport Bathurst has always been well served, but now it has a new branch of sport in which I honestly believe this city will produce champions as has been the case with football, cricket and tennis.

The late 1920s were hard years for most people but Bluey was already a focused and determined individual. The fine rider Les Wotton once said that a race against Bluey was never over until you crossed the line first. For all this, Wilkinson was able to listen, learn and get people on his side. Never ostentatious and always modest and calm, his general manner won most people over and endeared him to many. This, together with a burning desire to achieve and make his passion a reality, left few who met him doubting that he would succeed.

After that first meeting, young Arthur taught himself to ride a motorcycle. He was a fast learner. By the next speedway meeting in Bathurst, his application, talent and enthusiasm, honed on a borrowed machine and a number of tough informal contests, had made him good enough to compete. In preparation for the event he bought an ancient belt-driven Douglas machine for the princely sum of three pounds ten shillings; one pound deposit with five shillings a week repayments. However, the reports of his early exploits do not show the adolescent Wilkinson to be a speedway prodigy. Throughout October and November Bluey managed to do well in his heats, coming first or second. He made the semi-finals but there is no mention of him in the finals. This being the case, it was clear the young man had ability, but it leaves one suspecting that his machine was not quite up to the task of breaking through to the elite.

Bathurst quickly took to speedway and became one of the more popular tracks in Australia, both with riders and spectators. Thousands flocked to town for the meetings and men came from all over the continent to compete there. Bluey was able to learn from these gladiators, all the time adding to his skill and technique. It was not long before he took the mantle of local hero and favourite with the crowds. The district-wide interest in speedway racing attracted a number of local businessmen to become involved in promoting the sport. Bluey was noticed by one such entrepreneur from Orange, a Mr McMurtry who had a bike dealership. He offered to supply Bluey with a new Douglas racer in return for half his winnings. Wilkinson jumped at the deal and the new machine made a big difference. From December 1928, Bluey's performances began to show a definite upward turn. He was not only getting into finals but winning them! So Bluey learnt that a rider is only as good as his machine and he took the lesson to heart.

Opposite: Les Wotton.

Right: Clem Mitchell, New Cross.

Love thy Bike like Thyself

Although in his championship year he was racing so much that he took some help from Clem Mitchell, who worked alongside his own mechanic Len Stewart to keep his machines in prime condition, for most of his career Wilkinson tuned and checked his own bike. He would never go home to rest before he had checked over everything. He was fastidious about his machines. Nothing which could give him an extra ounce of speed was overlooked. 'Near enough' was never good enough. Every working part was fitted with artistic care, painstaking precision and consideration for all the variables. At any cost of time, patience and loss of sleep, he would arrive at the track with his motors inwardly perfect. But there were no outward signs of care; no painted and polished wheels, no bright shining handlebars, no decorations.

Working on his own machine, he built up a unique understanding of the motor. He knew by the feel, sound and smell of it what he needed to do and how to do it when it came to the match. In this way man and machine became one. It was no longer a case of one trying to get the other to bend to force or will. With the kind of familiarity Wilkinson fostered with his mount, rider and motor colluded and combined in contests against others, avoiding the accompanying personal battle between the organic and the mechanical. This took time to happen and was not achieved without injury and pain but the knowledge and confidence it gave Bluey made him able to do things that other riders could not begin to think about. He began to be known as a daring track performer. His ability and enthusiasm for the sport were apparent to the spectators and this fired them to believe in the young man and fuelled their want to see the local boy succeed.

Bluey's personable attitude helped him to get other people to do things for him. If he wanted special parts for his motor, he could always find some expert willing to spend hours tuning them up by hand for him. But he took pride and joy in tuning his own motors and believed all riders should do the same. For him a man who left his bike wholly with an employed mechanic was compromising his own professionalism and performance and maybe, as a consequence, the safety of himself and others.

Having it large with Van Praag

In December 1928 the great Lionel Van Praag accepted an invitation to race in Bathurst. Van Praag, who already had a reputation throughout Australia for being a tough, hard rider, was a star attraction and riders came from far afield to race against him. Local talent included Blos Blomfield and Harry Meyers but there was no mention of Bluey on this occasion.

Throughout January 1929 Bluey continued to win the 'A' Grade Handicap race on his home track. His chance to try his skill against Van Praag was to come on 11 February. *The Times of Bathurst* reported:

> *Although the weather was threatening and one or two sharp showers fell, a large crowd of speedway fans were present to witness the races on Saturday night. Sixth heat of the 'A' Grade Handicap was won by Wilkinson. The crowd was tense as Bluey lined up beside Van Praag for the second semi-final. A thrilling race began where Bluey threw his all into the attempt. He won and Van Praag had to take second place.*

The lad from the 'Queen City of the Plains' had gained his first success. But Bluey could not sustain his form. He had put so much into the semi-final that his machine let him down for the final and he was not even able to start with it.

Throughout March the reports of the speedway nights were including such praise as: 'Another rider to win popular approval during the night was Bluey Wilkinson. This boy is probably the most improved rider on the track at the moment and he displayed his skill to the utmost on Saturday night', and 'Bluey Wilkinson, Harry Meyers and Bios Blomfield have proved to be the best riders in Australia today'.

A career turning point for Bluey came on 8 April 1929; a second stab at Van Praag and a chance to show his first victory had been no fluke. This time there were to be no last-minute problems. Both riders made the final. A classic confrontation between the local young pretender and the kingpin was laid in place. The current daddy of the speedways of the southern hemisphere lined up against what was to be the future – Bathurst's Blue Boy. The start produced a huge roar, a combination of crowd and engine, the like of which had not been heard on the plains and that could be heard on sheep stations many miles away. The first two laps were tight, constituting a hard campaign wherein no-one was out of the running, the most dangerous and unpredictable eventualities in any race. As the riders crashed into the third lap Bluey pushed himself to hold the front position he had hung onto for much of the race. His machine raged and whined with the strain, but Lionel the Lion was not about to give way and lowered his head as they powered into the straight. But Bluey was in no mood to play a waiting game. It was blast or burst as far as he was concerned, something that was a feature of many of his rides as a younger man. As if taken on the winds of will he pulled away, crossing the finishing post with Van Praag fifty yards adrift. It was a notable and magnificent victory and a foretaste of the future. That an exceptional ride had been ridden, that this had been no lucky happening, was confirmed by the fact that Bluey set a new Australasian record for the mile over a quarter-mile track.

This awesome performance came almost at the end of the season in Australia and it was natural that such a success coming at that time would lead Bluey to think of a move to England, then the Mecca of speedway, where the new season was beginning to blossom. Friends tried to dissuade Bluey from the venture. He had been working with a local newspaper business and several people advised him to stick with this. However, as far as speedway was concerned, it seemed Wilkinson had gone as far as he could go in Australia. He had become the local wonder kid, not only beating the best his nation could offer but needing to give twenty-two-second starts in handicap events to make contests viable. Family and neighbours realized his potential and saw conviction. They started a fund to help him raise the fare to Britain. Just before he sailed from Freemantle his supporters presented him with a wallet containing £30.

Bluey's Australian feats had been reported on 3 April. He arrived at Tilbury on 2 May 1929. He was only seventeen years old, very young, particularly to be about as far from home as one might get. Together with his 'three tenners', he had left his homeland with a letter introducing him to Buzz Hibberd, an Australian riding for West Ham in East London. Hibberd met Bluey as the young man took his first steps on British soil. Almost immediately Buzz concluded that he liked the ginger-haired lad and wasted no time in taking the boy under his wing. He introduced Bluey to the West Ham management. At the time there were about fifty riders on the West Ham books and the Hammers boss wasn't too keen on taking on another Aussie. But Hibberd was not going to be put off and let it be known that he was ready to take his Australian gold, the tamer of Van Praag, to Claude Langton at Stamford Bridge. However, Aussie solidarity prevailed and Bluey became a Hammer. He was signed on but without the customary allowance for fares and expenses (Hibberd and of course Wilkinson were, at the time, ignorant of such perks). Other imports like Vic Huxley, Frank Arthur and Bill Lamont had received first-class fare and liberal expenses. The other Australians also had contracts which meant good money right from the start. Bluey never forgot or quite forgave this harsh and unfair treatment. However, West Ham had taken him on in unconventional circumstances. He was to become probably the only top-flight rider to come to Britain without any prior arrangements with agents or club representatives.

This was the start of Bluey's relationship with the West Ham club that was to last a decade. The season for speedway was already in full swing and the next morning the media covering speedway was proclaiming 'New Australian Champion Signs for West Ham'; 'Champion of Bathurst makes his debut at the Docklands track tomorrow night'. 'Bluey Wilkinson breaks records in practice'.

Frank Arthur.

When Bluey arrived in England, speedway was a new sport. It had been imported to England from Australia the previous year and there were still a number of organizational growing pains. Things seemed chaotic to people who had been around from the start. No one was really sure where the sport was going, so for Bluey it was all quite bewildering. Speedway had established itself, in a very short time, as a mass spectator sport and as such having huge money-making potential, at a time when the pre-Second World War depression was on the way. Speedway came at the right time and the right place. It was a form of escapism for people trapped in the throes of events over which they had no control. For as little as one shilling and threepence spectators could witness the daredevils of the track fighting it out. At that time the average working wage was two pounds five shillings a week for those lucky enough to be in employment. Some of the more famous riders were commanding fifty pounds for a single race. Although Wilkinson wouldn't be in this bracket for some time, he was to quickly learn that he not only had to be a rider but also a businessman as well.

Custom House, Canning Town, Plaistow, Silvertown and Stratford, the industrial villages of the Docklands that made up West Ham, were a stark contrast to New South Wales. Bluey had swapped heat for cold, the measured and open housing of Bathurst for the sprawling poverty of the clustered dwellings that made up the far East End of London. Wilkinson was brought up with a tennis court in his back garden, in a city where the air was freshened by breezes that blew across the green plains that

The Custom House Comet.

surrounded it, where sheep and cattle grazed. Most families in West Ham didn't have much more than a toilet in the backyard and were hemmed in by factories, warehouses, roads, railways, stockyards and docks. The evenings and mornings were dark. The sky, when it lightened, was grey and polluted, while the atmosphere was prone to be choked by deadly, lung-wrenching 'pea-soup' smog made up of the industrial and domestic filth of London, blown east by the prevailing winds and trapped over the docks.

However, Bluey was greeted warmly by the other Australian riders, teammates and opponents alike, who tended to watch out for the new arrivals and he managed to be included in one of the scratch races. Watching from the pits, it became obvious to the young man from Bathurst that this was all very different from meetings in his home town. Britain was at that time the meeting place of the world's great riders, men with massive experience and knowledge of the toughest of sports and a big and burgeoning business. Bluey observed and listened. He watched the riders elbowing each other, leaning over each other trying to round the corner first, touching wheels and handlebars; men and machines hit the dirt, metal and bone ground together. The arena at Custom House took its human and mechanical toll in a bevy of excitement, fear, adventure, ambition, fun, obsession and passion. It was a frightening and wonderful, awful and awesome world where one had to look at life full-on and live it to the utmost or else fail or even die. As his eyes bulged at it all and his brain worked to process what was before him, Arthur 'Bluey' Wilkinson was enveloped by his context. It now owned him as much as he adopted it. The world had turned and brought him into a mad, disordered, but strangely beautiful hell-on-earth. Now Bluey would start his life's work, to ride it, rule it and make it his paradise; many would share this heaven with him and love him for his efforts.

2

THE GIFT OF FOCUS

When he left Australia Bluey Wilkinson was a rider with exceptional potential but he did not have the innate abilities of many of the top men in the sport; the kind of extraordinary qualities of his countryman Vic Huxley, for instance. It is unfair to bracket Bluey Wilkinson with Huxley – they were very different riders but the Bathurst boy did learn from Vic and emulated Huxley's success in speedway. However, he wasn't another 'Hux' – any comparison would be spurious. Likewise, he couldn't be said to have the genius of Eric Langton, nor did he display the balance and poise of Jack Parker or the cold, killer instinct of Jack Milne. But Bluey was a born battler with the ability to concentrate and focus on a particular end. It was this, together an unshakable, perhaps passionate belief in himself, fabulous fitness, strength and exceptional bravery that made him an outstanding rider.

Looking at the West Ham programmes of 1929, Bluey is first mentioned in July of that year. He was riding under number 156 (all the racers had numbers and old programmes often have the rider numbers pencilled in). In the early stages of his career Bluey needed every ounce of his innate patience and resolve as he acclimatized to the tight tracks of England with their strange and unpredictable surfaces; he seemed always to be falling. As well as (and probably connected to this) he was often picked for the West Ham team and then dropped at the last moment. These were frustrating times for Bluey, but he always saw those first days in Britain as the making of him. Invariably success is the product of mistakes, but few of us actually learn from our mistakes, despite what the old adage would have us believe. We tend to make the same mistakes over and over again. However, our successes tend to arise out of our errors if we can learn to harness the factors that cause us to falter. This was something that Wilkinson did constantly.

As he developed, Bluey's style had much in common with Huxley's. Wilkinson neither trailed nor thrust his leg forward and appeared to make little if any use of it on corners. He developed the kind of balance that Huxley, Lamoreaux and Grosskreutz had as an innate quality. However, the broad, forward-moving, hunched shoulders and accompanying bulldog attitude became associated with Wilkinson as did a rare type of energy, a sort of tempered aggression, which existed in contrast to the ease with which

Eric Langton leads England at Belle Vue, 1932.

the other top riders rode their machines. Bluey's style never looked comfortable or even natural. To that extent he was like another Hammer, the great England soccer captain Bobby Moore – he made himself good. Bluey was 'self-produced'. His form came out of effort, preparation and a constant struggle to improve his speed. He made an almost scientific study of gate technique, developing more subtle methods of out-thinking and outflanking his opponents. If ever anyone wanted an example of a person's ability to make their own destiny, Bluey would be the ideal model.

3

A ROAR IN THE DOCKS

Friends, family and those who rode against him knew that from the moment Wilkinson left Australia for England his ambition was to be World Speedway Champion. However, he was understandably concerned about the expectations of him that the headlines which heralded his arrival at West Ham set in motion. It was clear to him that he had a lot to learn and do. However, the crowds were coming to see a new sensation, a champion from one of the birthplaces of speedway.

While speedway meetings had both drawn and satisfied the crowds, it was becoming clear that something more was required. This was recognised by the various promoters and the year 1929 saw the first attempt to put speedway racing on a proper and businesslike basis as the southern promoters put their heads together and formed the National Speedway Association to run the Southern League. Because it was felt that the top-grade riders would be too powerful for the general competition, it was decided to exclude them from League racing. These 'star' riders were to be financially compensated for their exclusion from league racing by receiving increased appearance money. The first sides to register teams for the League were Coventry, Crystal Palace, Hall Green (Birmingham), Harringay, Lea Bridge, Perry Barr (Birmingham), Southampton, Stamford Bridge, Wembley, White City and Wimbledon. Each team would race twenty matches, ten at home and ten away. The teams would consist of four riders and one reserve, with the riders riding in pairs over six heats, points being awarded on the basis of 4 points for the winner of a race, 2 points for second and 1 point for third place. The rest of the races at each meeting would follow the same format as in 1928 with a series of scratch and handicap races, match races and track-record attempts being held. This gave the sport a much-needed focus, giving whole areas an affinity to a stadium and a team. Teams were put together and organized by managers and so rider contracts were established and this resulted in payment becoming more reliable and regular. The first Custom House and London League match coincided with Bluey's arrival in England, taking place on 2 May 1929. Coventry were the visitors. In the West Ham side that day were Taffy Williams, Jack Adams, Les Maguire, Reg Bounds, Don Taylor, Buzz Hibberd the captain and Harold 'Tiger' Stevenson. Stevenson earned his nickname from his will to win regardless of seemingly

Above: Bluey Wilkinson, Tiger Stevenson, Tommy Croombs and Reg Bounds.

Opposite: Les Maguire.

endless accidents and crashes early on in his career. He also looked a bit like a tiger with his broad shoulders and handsome feline features. Stevenson was introduced to the finer points of riding by the American Lloyd 'Sprouts' Elder. Elder had a sweeping, quite spectacular style and Stevenson copied and developed this, even when more 'scientific' ways of riding evolved. Stevenson was to skipper West Ham through many battles and campaigns, but in this first skirmish the Hammers came out runaway winners, defeating the Midlanders 31-11.

With the coming of League racing, media interest grew and the *News of the World* sponsored the Southern League and put up a Challenge Cup for the winners of the competition as well as presenting substantial cash prizes to the members of the winning team.

The first few times Bluey wheeled his machine into the West Ham pits he took time out to watch the star riders. Bill Lamont, Roger Frogley, Colin Watson and Sprouts Elder. The American was the king of the track, with a string of shining new machines and attendants to carry his gear. He had all the trappings of a man earning anything from £300 to £600 a week, a huge amount of money in 1929. Like any other young man in his position the rookie Aussie was intimidated.

Racing Sprouts

One of Bluey's first contests at Custom House was a scratch race. In time it became something of a tradition at West Ham to follow the team racing with a scratch race for a prize. Bluey was to cut his teeth on the English tracks in such races. He had watched the racing with the riders jostling at full speed as they took the bends. The whole thing

Tiger on the loose.

took on a dramatic tinge lit up in the glare of the track's arc lamps. It was very aggressive racing compared with his previous experience. When the riders returned to the pits their faces were black with combat and their eyes full of cinders and dirt. They were sweating and gasping, near to exhaustion. Some nearly fell as they dismounted, others shouted and swore, either in elation or protest. Every time a man was beaten it hit his pride, his heart and his wallet and so a world of anger, bitterness and often massive disappointment was provoked.

The pit marshal's call came and Bluey began his final preparations. He tugged the straps of his helmet, adjusted his steel-soled shoe and wheeled his machine to the pit gate. The speakers announced his entry, 'In the next race we have our new Australian discovery. Give him a hand folks!' There was a murmur of anticipation from the crowd. Not all the Australians who had come to West Ham had been a success and there was a feeling among some that they were edging out local talent. To Bluey the 40,000 fans were menacing. But his powerful twin-engine Douglas purred under him and gave him some assurance. Four hungry-looking riders on huge, dominating mechanical monsters rolled round the quarter-mile track together closing in like predators on the starter's flag. In those days the West Ham track was no more than thirty feet wide down the straights. A rider needed nerves of steel to fly four abreast at top speed along this confined space. A helmeted figure appeared on Bluey's right; another on his left, a third was just behind. The front three pairs of handlebars seemed to be almost touching. They rolled gently round the bend into the straight and then, as they saw the starter move into position, the pack accelerated. They gathered momentum and began to find speed. As they passed the starter, the four were moving near to sixty miles per hour. The race was on.

Bluey was riding number three position. His thoughts were dominated with the intent on getting round the corner first. He had convinced himself this was what he needed to do as he would have to impose himself or become an also-ran. The corner rushed at him at such a speed he felt the shock. He was still not used to his new home track and although it was big in comparison to many British ovals, it felt tight as the crowd bore down on the riders at the turns. His face was flushed and his eyes were straining with the exhilaration and this seemed to enhance his peripheral vision. He saw the man on the inside drifting in towards him. Before there was time to think, let alone panic, their elbows touched and an instant later their knees crunched together. He was now in danger of being scuttled in front of his first real home crowd. Now it was either push back or take some kind of evasive action. Not having much option Bluey edged towards the fence. Amazingly his foe followed. Possibilities were narrowing. Wilkinson was in more danger if he shut off, so he held on grimly and hoped for the best. Everything was tight as they flashed round the bend. One false move would mean disaster. At the speed they were making, anything out of unison would mean certain and instant carnage. Somehow the bend was cleared, which for a fraction of a second took the pressure off. But as they straightened up the rush down the back straight began. Surrounded by a blurred sea of speed Bluey felt someone pass him on the inside. He felt a vicious spray of cinders full in the face and was blinded momentarily. His face stung and smarted, but instinctively he drove on, through the pain and

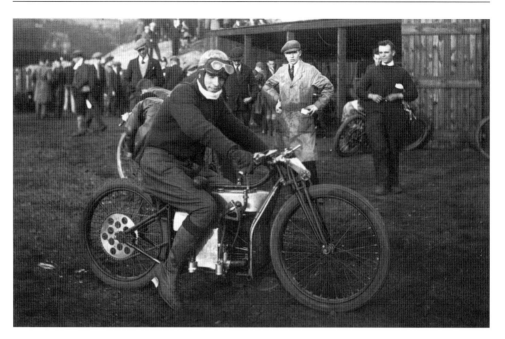

Sprouts Elder.

mounting turmoil. Wilkinson felt the control of his machine come back to him and without a thought, working totally on primal urge, ripped the useless goggles from his face. He felt a sudden loss of speed; what was happening? Another man in a white jacket drew alongside. They raced down the straight wheel to wheel, grimly determined, tense and fervent. Bluey decided to keep the taps open as long as his opponent did. The safety fence with its steel mesh and tough guard rail haunted him like a ghoul and it was coming right at him. Thirty yards ahead he saw the man who had passed him fall. Too much too soon. Having pulled back some power the 'Bathurst Blur' was on fire and moving fast, and beside him was a big, heavy-footed, driven man who was not going to give way. This was madness! Was he in front, second? Bluey was lost in the race and there was nothing to do but race.

Wilkinson knew that the sensible thing to do would be to pull up, but if he did his opponent might not do the same thing. For all this, pressing on put the mortality of himself, the rider on his shoulder and the faller in the balance. The situation seemed to take over and he saw that while the decked rider lay directly in his path, his uncontrolled machine was screaming, still at full throttle, bouncing about the track. If Bluey kept going it seemed he would be 'over the motor' or 'over the man'. There seemed to be no space between the prostrate rider, the fallen bike and the fence. Each way pointed towards calamity.

At the last minute the young Hammer saw a space open and as the stranded machine spun he set himself to make the gap his own. The enclosure gasped in relief as Bluey went through the finishing line with a hundred yards to spare. He came home the winner. His run for safety and his refusal to pull back in the face of seeming fate had carried him to victory. He'd won his first race in Britain, beating the legendary American Sprouts Elder. Maybe he wouldn't have won if the man had not fallen and Bluey had certainly thought he was going through the fence, but for all this, destiny had been with him and made him the victor. Apart from this the whole experience had been amazing, something he could never see himself giving up. He realised that this was the feeling he had been born for.

Victor Nelson Huxley

The meeting went on with more falls, collisions and accidents. Ambulance men were rushing round all night. Then it was the semi-final. Wilkinson didn't have much chance of winning because the champion of all the champions was in the race, Brisbane's genius Victor Nelson Huxley. Although seemingly a daring rider, Huxley never had Bluey's problems with staying on board his bike.

The semi-finalists were announced and the riders rolled round to the start. Bluey wasn't lucky in terms of the draw. He started on the outside while Huxley got the inside. The first effort to get the race underway resulted in a false start. This was a common occurrence in the early days of the sport, until Fred Mockford's starting gate was introduced. Bikes held just enough fuel to race the distance so false starts often meant that riders had to refuel, thus causing delays and crowd frustration, which was already high because the inequality of the motors meant that races were becoming predictable. Men with fast machines just drew away from their opponents on slower bikes. The stars were not risking any learner getting the jump on them and then probably falling in front of them. Starting positions made a difference too. Bluey, being on the outside, would need to try and ride round fast men who were hugging the line; this would be an almost impossible task. The general theory of racing was to drive fast for the corner, then to shut back for a brief second. Timing being everything, the lull would be followed by a powerful dive for the line, jockeying a way through the crowd of riders with the same thing in mind. Bluey knew nothing of these tactics but even if he had known he was far too inexperienced to have successfully timed and carried out the necessary manoeuvres. As it was he simply charged blindly on with a big handful of twist grip. He was up with Huxley at the drop of the flag, only to find, a split second later, that he was yards behind his compatriot. For all this, Bluey decided to hang on as long as possible and watch points. It was an experience like no other he had been through. Huxley took him into the corner so fast he couldn't get his motor round; it wouldn't steer and he found himself on the ground with over two hundred pounds of screaming jumping bike rebelling against him. However, intuitively Wilkinson had held on to his handlebars and was able to pull himself and his machine upright. He collected a shower of cinders as a rider flashed past and then another as he ran with his machine. He leapt back into the saddle and chased the field. The nearest man was the length of the straight away, but to the surprise of the watching fans Bluey was after the consolation of a place. According to the rules of the track at that time, once a rider was lapped he was out of the race. As such Bluey had to ride flat out. Races like this were not uncommon in the late twenties. The unexpected was always happening in this embryonic sport. Huxley bore down swiftly on the struggling novice. He didn't

Vic Huxley, Wimbledon, July 1935.

want to pass the boy and rob him of his meagre place winnings, however the other riders behind him were pressing. One tried to pass, careless of the lad's earnings. 'Hux' opened his throttle and shifted his position, which made his back wheel fire a barrage of cinders that caused the assailant to swerve straight into the safety fence and out of the race. The fourth rider wobbled and fell while trying to avoid the crash, but he jumped up and started wheeling his machine, which refused to start, to the finishing post only a length of the straight away. Bluey was oblivious to all this. He was too busy riding as if his life depended on the outcome. Passing the pit gates he caught a fleeting glimpse of the other riders waving him on. He looked round, generally something of a sin in the sport, and took in the situation. He had almost three quarters of a lap to ride. Could he catch the running man before he completed the few yards to the post? Bluey rode recklessly into the corner, struggled around and saw he still had a chance. He leaned forward and opened the throttle wide and smashed down the straight. He could see the figure with the chequered flag held high, ready to drop it for him or the perspiring runner who was now nearly exhausted but still struggling forward. Just a yard from the finish the sprinter fell and Bluey grabbed second place. From that moment on the West Ham crowd recognised Wilkinson as a trier and loved him for it.

The Way of the Track

The advent of team racing changed the whole atmosphere of speedway racing. Individuals had been the attraction but from 1929 the crowds would come to support their teams. But it was made quite clear that only winning riders would be in the side. Losers were dropped. However, only those chosen for the team could make any money. Before 1929, star riders had been paid booking fees from £10 to £100 per meeting and some of them raced six or more times a week. The majority of the riders had never earned more than fifty shillings a week before they took up racing and some had come straight from school. This prize money was unbelievable wealth to them. The careful ones saved, the spendthrifts were little better off. Big cars, nightclubs and gambling took the hard-won cash of many a rider as well as sweeter temptations. Women were attracted to speedway more than any other sport and the young men who rode the tracks were as attracted to them. The ovals of Britain were full of dangers, some more obvious than others. The lesser lights, among whom was Wilkinson, rode for a £3 booking fee and all they could win, which was not a lot. To lose a motor was a dire calamity.

Bluey was beginning to take the odd race from top riders, victories which for the most part were taken as acts of impertinence by a junior rider. He often achieved such feats carrying the effects of injury, filled up with half the track, having been squeezed hard up against the fence, and then passing a star in the last few yards. Although he had mastered some of the tricks of the back-wheel slide and a managed to stop his front wheel running away from under him, he was still falling, due mostly to both wheels slipping about on greasy surfaces. He found himself facing Frank Charles, the then Wembley champion, who was later killed in a glider accident. Frank was a wonderful rider but had a bad habit of looking back over his shoulder. The race went the whole four laps; however Bluey just couldn't get through. Every now and then Frank would snap his head round to see where the rest of the field were. Bluey figured it out that if he got close enough to Charles and far enough to the inside of him he would be able to get out of Frank's line of vision. The tactic worked like a dream. Bluey made his move coming out of the last bend and just managed to get the verdict. It was the boast of most of the top riders of Bluey's era that they were familiar with the riding style and racing technique of most of their opponents. Some looked back from under their arms. One rider might take the occasional glance over his left shoulder; another might check things out to his right, a few riders hardly ever bothered to check out what was happening behind them. There were riders who would hesitate and lose speed if challenged by a sudden attack and men who would try to steer clear of the fence, being anxious about being pushed or sucked into it. On the other hand there were as many who avoided the inner edge. Some individuals could be relied upon to never attempt to pass another except on the inside and others stuck strictly to the outside when overtaking. One or two were frightened to pass at all and tried to hold their place from the start; if they got in front they would fight like fury to stay there but if they were passed they were content with the places. There were a few riders who had the habit of menacingly drifting towards other riders if they tried to overtake them, but oddly they would allow an opponent by on the inside. Others did just the opposite. There were men who would fight for every inch at one meeting and seem to lose their fire at

Frank Charles.

another event. Then there were the consistent battlers who would never give ground and do everything in their power to gain it. Bluey was most positively in this bracket.

Shoot-out at Custom House

During the writing of this book I spoke to a number of former West Ham riders and many former supporters of the team and, while all knew of Bluey Wilkinson, few recalled watching him ride. However, my grandmother sold programmes at Custom House right from the start of racing there and my grandfather spent some time working as a pusher and raker. They lived with my dad in Churchill Road, Custom House. The home of West Ham speedway was just at the bottom of their street. They both used to tell me about those early days of speedway, just after my dad was born. My grandfather was particularly impressed with how hard Bluey worked in the early stages of his track career. He told me how although he was not always able to make the West Ham team, he was continuously racing, taking opportunities offered at any track. This learning by doing began to pay off and he started to take one or two significant scalps, but this had its downside. As a rider built his reputation he was as much the hunted as he was the hunter and, as my granddad told me, the defeat of Sprouts Elder made him the object of some American attention. On more than one occasion he told me tales of the other two big Yank names of that era, Art Pecher and Ray Tauser (who won the Star National Speedway Championship while with Wimbledon in 1931) and how they went looking for Bluey.

The programmes and the journals of the early days of speedway didn't always get the facts right, indeed Bluey, like most other riders of the era, rode in many more races than were ever recorded. The consequence of this is that many wonderful confrontations have been lost and only live on in folk memory. I just don't know if what I am about to relate was ever written down, although I do recall my grandfather reading me an account of events from a tattered newspaper-like document as a sort of bedtime story. Anyway, according to both my grandparents an Aussie/Yank showdown took the shape of one of those almost informal scratch events that happened at West Ham at the dawn of speedway, wherein the competitors were often finalized on the evening. On this night at Custom House in the early part of the 1930s there was some decent prize money on offer, which had attracted a good field. Granddad, who would often chat to riders, told me that Wilkinson was aware of the two men either side of him at the start of the race that brought them together. Bluey instinctively felt their need to prove a point, as if the bare desire to win was not enough; there was a taste of revenge in their burning dope.

Bluey got a bit of a jump at the start and pulled close into the line and held position for the first two laps, all the time being stalked by the American posse. As they charged into the third orbit Pecher drew level at the corner and began to lean on the diminutive redhead. Tauser was hugging close behind to cover any eventualities. But Bluey was in no mood to be intimidated. Keeping his throttle open, he let his machine drift and took Pecher with him. This made room on the inside which Tauser grabbed in an instant. The first corner of the final lap cradled the three riders in unison and they burst into the back straight as one. Locked wheel to wheel it all began to look dangerous. Pecher was the first to break, going wide with the intention of diving across Bluey at the next turn, an all or nothing manoeuvre, which reeked of disaster for all three combatants, but to Pecher's mind this may have been preferable to allowing the Aussie to humble two more Americans in one fell swoop. However, Bluey had read the situation and guessed the plan. He ran the line as a tightrope walker might embrace the wire path. Wilkinson had to hang on! Halfway down the straight Bluey felt something touch his trailing foot and knew it was Tauser's front wheel. He was in a kind of three-way sandwich between the two Yanks and the line; there was one way out only and that was forward, but to open that gate he needed speed. He would have to gamble everything into the penultimate turn and hit the corner faster than he had ever let himself. He also had to go in tight, but not too tight, as the resulting crash would be nothing but carnage. Tauser saw sense and declined to follow the rush into the bend, but here Pecher saw his chance to crush Bluey by cutting in deep. But all Bluey would have to do was match his speed to stay clear. However, Pecher had space where Bluey had hope. Straining every muscle Wilkinson pushed down on his machine and into the bend. It looked like an impossible angle that threw up shale and smoke like a terrible hell-storm from the like of which only Satan might emerge. The vast Custom House crowd was, for a long second, completely silent, but they roared as Bluey came hurtling out of grim, dense cloud well in the lead, to the extent that he was able to ease into the last bend for the final charge. However, Pecher had not given up and no more than twenty yards from the finish he had caught the dour young Aussie. 'It's never over till it's over' he shouted through the mighty bellows of the race. They flashed over the line. Confusion reigned for what seemed like an age. Everyone was speculating on the outcome. Those nearest the finish swore Wilkinson had got home first but the majority of the spectators, including Tauser, who was slapping his compatriot on the back from the moment they had joined each other after crossing the line, were convinced Pecher had regained America's honour. The noble Yank was the first to congratulate Bluey when the result was finally announced. Initially, Tauser, hand on hips, hung his head, but then he joined the other two men in handshakes. In the end speedway riders were a nation unto themselves and the race the ultimate winner.

The Struggle Continued

Bluey's potential was obvious but he was still falling often and although he seemed to steer clear of serious injuries, perhaps because of his low centre of gravity (he was not much more than five feet tall), he was kept on by West Ham mainly because of his promise. In his initial months in British speedway, Bluey was constantly encouraged by Hibberd and he doubled up as a mechanic so his frequent spills were more easily accepted as a symptom of his acclimatization to the wide range and varying quality of racing tracks and surfaces of the Southern League. However, by degrees, the newcomer grew in confidence and technical ability and his rides in the West Ham League side became increasingly more frequent. West Ham finished their first League season in sixth place, trailing well behind Stamford Bridge, who dominated the competition, winning all but three of their twenty matches.

1929 Southern League

Team	PL	W	D	L	Pts
Stamford Bridge	20	17	0	3	34
Southampton	20	16	0	4	32
Coventry	20	14	0	6	28
Crystal Palace	20	11	0	9	22
Wembley	20	11	0	9	22
West Ham	20	8	0	12	16
White City	20	8	0	12	16
Harringay	20	7	0	13	14
Birmingham	20	7	0	13	14
Lea Bridge	20	6	0	14	12
Wimbledon	20	5	0	15	10

Birmingham were originally named Perry Barr, as there was also another Birmingham team at that time called Hall Green who eventually dropped out after only a few meetings in 1929.

1929 Northern League

Team	PL	W	D	L	Pts
Leeds	23	17	1	5	35
Preston	24	16	0	8	32
Halifax	22	14	1	7	29
Rochdale	24	12	1	11	25
Leicester (Blackbird Rd)	23	10	1	12	21
Salford	21	10	0	11	20
Liverpool	21	10	0	11	20
Sheffield	21	8	1	12	17
Newcastle	18	8	0	10	16
Barnsley	21	8	0	13	16
Middlesbrough	21	6	0	15	12

White City (Manchester) resigned in September due to a dispute. At that point they had a record of 36 points from 18 matches and were undefeated. In the same month Warrington were expelled for an infringement with a record of 11 points from 18 matches.

Belle Vue and Burnley had previously resigned in July, probably because of the poor organization of the League.

Matches in 1929 were originally decided over six heats, but in June it was extended to nine. Each race was scored on a 4-3-2-1 point system with four riders making up the team.

The speedway season in England began after Easter and continued until October. When League racing started the first thing Bluey did was to bank enough to pay his fare home to Australia. The results he needed to support himself and pay for the care and maintenance of his machine did not come and he was obliged to use his fare money and thus face the winter in Britain. Bluey had a hard time in the cold of England and the winter of 1929 was bitterly cruel. Most of the overseas riders left in November for Australia or America. Other men survived either by pooling their savings or doing a bit of trading or taking jobs as garage hands at very low wages. But with the depression kicking in, jobs were hard to come by and the months of his first close season were some of the hardest of Wilkinson's life. Bluey was never to forget that winter. He learnt the value of money. When he was earning from £40 to £140 a week he became a conservative and prudent person in terms of his financial dealings. From 1930 Wilkinson made sure that he had enough finances to take the boat for Australia and race for three months down under. He was a very popular rider in Australia and at one time had thirty-eight consecutive wins on the Sydney track, the place where his mentor and friend had lost his life a year earlier. It is sad that Buzz Hibberd was never to see the success of his protégé. Hibberd was killed while wintering in Australia in 1929. His machine had seized solid and a fraction of a second later he was struck from behind by another rider and killed instantly. Bluey lost another friend in that early part of his career when another Aussie, Con Cantwell, died racing in Belgium.

His enforced stay in England during the winter of 1929 did allow Bluey to make preparations for 1930. As the new season drew near, money had to be found to maintain his bike and if he was to race from one end of the country to the other, he required a means to transport his bike, tools and himself. His taste, together with the limitations of his wallet produced a massive Buick. He paid five pounds for it and it was a good car. The brakes wouldn't work and the tyres were showing white here and there but the body was good if a little battered fore and aft. Perhaps it would have been advisable to have taxed and insured the monster, but the engine was first rate and he drove the beast for thousands of miles before abandoning it 'dead' on the Great West Road. He bought another model with quite a turn of speed and this cost him £15. For another tenner he got a trailer. Even with this pulling along behind, few cars ever passed Bluey. He would often drive all night at high speed and, on reaching his destination, be obliged to get his own machines ready for the next evening before he had any rest.

The sport was still by no means secure; tracks were known to fold overnight. But Bluey began to accumulate some money in the bank and he was starting to be something of an attraction because of his daring style and courage. Crowds had started to recognise his hunched shoulders, his powerful concentration and massive determination, and many adored and admired him. At various points it looked as if Bluey might be transferred from West Ham and certainly the likes of Johnnie Hoskins at Wembley were ready to come in for him. However, the length of the Custom House track suited him and the surface, being deep in wet, black cinders also complimented his 'do-or-die' style. To get caught in the backlash of the flying dirt as it left the whirring wheels of a speeding bike when broadsiding around the corners, was decidedly unpleasant. Only the tough ones survived the ordeal. Week after week new riders came

The Wembley team, 1929. From left to right: Jack Ormston, Johnnie Hoskins (manager), Buster Frogley, Harry Whitfield, Bert Fairweather, Len Reeve.

onto the speedway only to quit when they found out how hard and unforgiving the game was. But Wilkinson stuck with it. His constant falls led to him being advised by management to try for second placings for a while. Typically he refused, not willing to 'take dirt' from anyone.

In those days there was one big bath for all the riders. First in got the clean water, last in sat on the foundation of soapsuds and cinders. Often it was uproar with twenty or so young men wrestling, laughing and splashing in two feet of water. Most would be in pain at the same time from wounds picked up on the track. At this time unemployment was rife – those who made it in speedway were a world apart. Not one of them was earning less than five pounds a night and some were getting as much as fifty pounds for a single evening of riding. The big stars were getting nearer £200-300. As such, a day off to nurse an injury would be had at a huge cost, so most riders tended to try and ignore such occupational hazards and although he was improving, Bluey was still taking more spills than most, enough for the press to make his tumbles the focus of many reports. This seemed to endear him to supporters and overall the lad from Bathurst was making satisfactory progress.

However, in one ten-pound race Bluey was comfortably in front when there was a tearing of metal and an explosion. His crank-case flew apart and bits of his only machine flew over the track. He took a toss and was winded for a minute. When he recovered he found his machine was a wreck. Bluey realised that without a motor he was going nowhere, so he withdrew. He needed to buy a new engine, which would mean an outlay of £60 and he only had £50 in the bank, his fare home. Freddy Dixon, the genial, big-hearted motor racer, who at the time was with Douglas Motors, had a spare machine and let Bluey have it for £50 cash and the balance on credit. He negotiated a second engine, making an arrangement with West Ham for weekly payments. Now Bluey was in debt and this put him in battle mood. All he had in the world were two motors and his potential, and he was going to realize it. However, the first outing on his new bike riding against Wembley did not go well. The machine was awkward to steer and difficult on corners but it did have a good turn of speed; he couldn't acclimatize and found himself dropped from the side. Nevertheless, he had to continue to ride, to stay in speedway and get out of England before the winter. To Bluey he was riding for his life. However, out of his endeavour in desperation came his salvation. One night Bluey took yet another fall. It was a bad one and he was unconscious for quite a time. When he came round, perhaps understandably, his first question was about the state of his motor. His left handlebar was bent and the stewards tried to dissuade him from riding in the next race but to no avail. He had to race! Race he did and to everyone's amazement he won. He decided his bent handlebar was the secret of his success and from then on he rode with the modification, and his riding improved.

Out of Adversity, Success

The bent handlebar wasn't the whole secret of Bluey's success. He had a great admiration for Vic Huxley and had plenty of opportunity to watch his style. He developed a technique of his own modelled on Vic's method, but as time passed, Bluey contrived a very distinctive riding characteristic. His almost perfect sense of balance became the feature of his riding. He wasn't a natural, he had to thrust his broad shoulders forward and really work at it.

Arthur Wilkinson was, in the last part of the 1930 season, coming to be recognized as potentially one of the best riders in the country. His unorthodox style and indomitable spirit, frequently winning by sheer persistence and will, caused him to stand out among his peers and, as in all sport, recognition blended with talent is everything. His finances reflected his growing prowess and he was able to get back to Australia for the winter. But he still had a long way to go to catch his countryman Vic Huxley. In 1930 Huxley won eight major championships and a score of other prizes. Prize money for these was usually about £100, which was big money almost eighty years ago, but Vic's winnings for the year were well over £5,000, a substantial ransom in 1930. He was possibly for a time the highest-paid sportsman in the world.

Hammers Hammering

West Ham nominated Sprouts Elder (Overseas) and Ivor Creek (England) for the Star Riders' Championship. This was the pre-1936 equivalent of the World Championship, sponsored by the *London Star* newspaper. It existed to establish who was the best individual rider of the day. From 1930 the contestants were drawn from the top twelve scorers from the first 15 league matches of the season. Three riders at a time lined up in eliminating races culminating in a run-off between two riders.

Sprouts Elder won his first-round match, defeating Southampton's Billy Galloway. However, in the semi-final, Vic Huxley simply outclassed the American. Ivor Creek was beaten by the man who would win the event, Roger Frogley, in the second round, having taken Tommy Croombs, a Hammer to be but at that time with Lea Bridge, in the first round. Croombs was a diminutive and shy person. Before taking to the cinders, first with Brighton and then Lea Bridge (where he took the track record in 1928) he had worked in New Malden as a plasterer. After two years at Lea Bridge the strong, silent Croombs joined Bluey and the rest of the Custom House boys to become a legendary Hammer.

After 1930 it was clear that West Ham were a potent growing force in speedway. They had strong support and a developing squad of riders. There is little doubt that Bluey was in the right place at the right time. London was still very much the centre of Britain, its Empire and the world. The city was also the hub of British sport, when Britannia still ruled the waves and could confidently boast of being the mightiest sporting nation on the face of the earth. London was the place sporting stars needed to be. There were other powerful speedway teams in the capital but only Wembley could compete in terms of numbers and none could match the kind of loyalty and enthusiasm of the West Ham fans. There is a Cherokee chant that goes back to the days when the white man first started to oppress the indigenous Americans. Roughly translated it says:

> *There are drums beyond the mountains,*
> *Indian drums that you can't hear;*
> *There are drums beyond the mountains,*
> *And they're getting mighty clear.*

Something similar might be related to East London as the autumnal sun set on the river in 1930. There was a roaring in the docks; a thunder made by humans and machines. Bluey Wilkinson and the mighty Hammers were coming.

Opposite: Vic Huxley.

Right: Tommy Croombs.

Below: Ivor Creek.

1930 Southern League

Team	PL	W	D	L	Pts
Wembley	24	20	1	3	41
Southampton	24	17	1	6	35
Stamford Bridge	24	16	1	7	33
Wimbledon	24	16	1	7	33
Birmingham	24	13	1	10	27
Coventry	24	13	1	10	27
Crystal Palace	24	11	1	12	23
Lea Bridge	24	10	1	13	21
West Ham	24	10	0	14	20
Leicester (Blackbird Rd)	24	8	1	15	17
High Beech	24	8	0	16	16
Harringay	24	7	0	17	14
Nottingham	24	2	1	21	5

The invincible Vic Huxley, skipper of Harringay, took fifty-two lap records on the thirty-five tracks he competed on and had won nine £100 competitions. Vic was then earning around £200–£300 per week. Birmingham competed this season at Hall Green rather than Perry Barr.

1930 Northern League

Team	PL	W	D	L	Pts
Belle Vue	21	19	1	1	39
White City (Manchester)	15	13	0	2	26
Liverpool	18	13	0	5	26
Preston	15	8	0	7	16
Warrington	17	8	0	9	16
Sheffield	13	6	0	7	12
Leicester (Melton Rd)	13	4	1	8	9
Edinburgh	11	4	0	7	8
Barnsley	12	4	0	8	8
Newcastle	9	2	0	7	4
Wombwell	12	2	0	8	4
Rochdale	10	2	0	8	4
Glasgow White City	11	2	0	9	4

The season was remembered as a fiasco, with many teams completing less than half their fixtures. The victorious Belle Vue side included Frank Varey, Arthur Franklyn, Eric and Oliver Langton, Dusty Haigh and Bob Harrison.

On Sunday 29 June a number of riders, masked to avoid recognition, staged a meeting at the Audenshaw trotting track in Lancashire without an ACU licence. Over 12,000 paid to enter while an estimated 5,000 got in for free after crashing the barriers. As a result, thirty-four riders and nine officials were suspended.

Right: Frank Varey.

4

BLOOMIN' BLUEY

Bluey Wilkinson was part of a wave of Australian experience and know-how that fed, sustained and helped develop speedway in Britain. By the start of the 1930s Britain was firmly established as the centre of world speedway and was pulling crowds as big – and at times bigger – than any other sport, including football. However, it was the Australians who were dominating the tracks. Even experienced riders like Sprouts Elder had gone back to America, having been pushed to the sidelines by the influx of young competition. However, some British riders found a place in the top flight, Buster and Roger Frogley being among the best of them, but early records indicate the Australians were, in the main, unmatched.

Fan-tastic!

Unlike other mass spectator sports in the 1930s, speedway meetings were family events. People of all ages attended and at West Ham there seemed to be as many women fans as there were male. When the Hammers rode at other tracks they took a huge following with them and were probably the best-supported away side in the League. The fans, with scarves, whistles, rattles, crossed-hammer badges and banners, let everyone know they were there. Long before their football counterparts, West Ham fans were singing their songs of support and inventing chants to let the riders know they were behind them. While there was severe rivalry between sides, particularly when local rivals visited, there was no hate and no one can ever recall a 'speedway hooligan'. The tracks always seemed to be places of joy and fun. Being mostly a summer sport, it took place on some long, hot nights. Girls and boys had a good excuse to be out relatively late and the West Ham track was the site of many a romance, some serious courting and the root of not a few marriages. The mass support was encouraged by an admission charge of sixpence, by far and away the lowest asked for by any major side. West Ham had a massive supporters' club, with around 500 members who had paid two shillings to join this esteemed group, getting a claret and blue enamel badge, entitlement to admission to a range of social events, entry to the enclosures for less than half the normal price and reduced admission at away tracks.

Left: Hammer man Croombs.

Opposite: Tiger Stevenson, West Ham captain.

The 1930 season was West Ham's second of its three as part of the Southern League. Jimmy Baxter was in overall charge and Arthur Elvin came in as promoter, while Alec Jackson was appointed speedway manager.

Hammerin' On

Having 'made hay' in the initial boom period, many of the stars of the first couple of years of organized speedway chose to hang up their leathers, not really having the appetite for team racing. In 1931 Tiger Stevenson and Bluey Wilkinson were the only survivors from the side that had completed the previous season. Tiger was an outside man with only one speed, wide open: win or hit the dirt seemed to be his riding philosophy. As such, it was always a spectacle to see him ride. Once, on a three-mile track in Sydney, he hit sixty on one wheel for almost the length of a straight. Stevenson and Wilkinson rode for some time as partners in the early League matches. They often carried the team, particularly when Tommy Croombs was injured. When Exeter was running, this was a favourite hunting ground for the 'Blur' and the 'Tiger'. It was a banked cycle track around a football ground and when the riders cut loose on this cinder path it looked like sheer suicide.

Bluey and Tiger were joined at Custom House by Tommy Croombs, Arthur Westwood, Allen Kilfoyle, Bert Jones and Don Durant, and the side looked firm enough. However, such a massive change of personnel was bound to have

Tommy Croombs, riding for
Empire Speedways, 1936/37.

consequences and West Ham were unable to really gel as a side, finishing ninth after the final League match. Stamford Bridge had put paid to the Hammers' hopes in the London Cup (The *London Evening News* launched the London Cup in 1930) in the first round, but the East Enders grabbed the Essex County Championship, defeating High Beech home and away and beating Lea Bridge at Custom House. Tiger Stevenson made it to the Star Riders' Championship final as one the League's top-twelve point takers. He was also picked for England in the third Test match against Australia at Stamford Bridge; Bluey Wilkinson was with the Aussie side.

Tommy Gunning

Tommy Croombs had a meteoric rise as a scratch starter in handicap races and was easy to pick out because of his habit of almost standing on his right footrest when going into turns, not unlike the great Frank Arthur. Again like Arthur, even going flat out, he tended to hug the white line, so much so he was given the moniker 'The White-Line Wizard'. He would take hold on the inside position and then set out to pursue the field – he loved the chase and never felt entirely happy in front. Tommy would often twist in close behind his opponent and then proceed to wipe his front wheel on his competitor's foot. If this failed to persuade the other rider to move out a bit, he would ram the wheel up under his knee. In not a few final-heat dramas, Croombs and Wilkinson would steal the evening by the use of cunning team strategies, one taking the inside, the other holding the outside, leaving their opponent trapped in the gap with few options.

Charlie Spinks.

Tommy Croombs didn't make the best of starts at his new club. He left a couple of toes on the track after catching his foot in the chain, then he broke a collarbone in a fall. When he got back from that he got in another toss and broke the other collarbone. He also collected minor injuries, sprains, bruises and cuts. His tumbles were not at all in character. Tommy was a fine rider and something of a rarity among the top English competitors, having mastered the Peashooter Harley.

Peashooter, Douglas, Rudge and Chains

The Harley-Davidson Peashooter was developed especially for board-track racing and it was readily adapted to circuit racing in Australia, which first became a mass draw in the Newcastle area of New South Wales. The Peashooter was, for a long time, the only bike specifically designed for the sport. Probably more than any other machine, it was the pioneering bike of Australian dirt-track racing and most of the top Australian riders of the 1930s including Charlie Spinks, Vic Huxley and Frank Charles, began their careers on the Peashooter. In the 350cc capacity range they were clearly superior to anything else for many years. Later machine designs, right up to the contemporary period, have clearly been influenced by the Peashooter.

Although riders like Huxley, Spinks and Charles often took corners with the throttle wide open on the Peashooter, it had a cut-out button mounted on the left handlebar. The throttle was not easy to control in any other position but wide open; in consequence, speed and control often relied on the use of the cut-out button rather than the throttle. One bold exponent of cut-off-button use was Charlie 'Daredevil'

Spinks. As his moniker suggests, Charlie was one of the most audacious riders of the early days of speedway and was known for his habit of actually stepping off in impossible situations using the cut-off button.

The British Individual Championship

League racing really spoilt the British public's appetite for handicaps and scratch races and it was clear that 'ongoing' competition had the mass appeal. The British Individual Championship facilitated this while preserving the individual competition that was embedded in the culture of speedway. The Individual Championship was open only to the top riders (the first championship was only open to Southern League riders – Northern League riders were only allowed to enter after the founding of the National League in 1932). Colin Watson, then captain of Wembley, and Vic Huxley where the first to fight it out. Their race at West Ham saw Huxley take the honours.

This Individual Championship was one of the top prizes speedway could offer. Every track had at least one rider qualified to race for the title but obviously everybody could not ride. There was a feeling among some riders that the bigger tracks were keeping the Individual Championship to themselves because of the huge gates it attracted. The control board selected those able to ride for the title but with two promoters on the board, questions were asked.

Revving Reg

Stevenson, Wilkinson, Croombs and Kilfoyle were consistently in the West Ham side from the beginning of the 1931 season. Con Cantwell, Frank Randall, Reg and Cecil Bounds also made the team. Reg Bounds was to be among the top League points winners of that year. He also took the Essex Championship and won a couple of Test caps, racking up ten points during the third Test at Wembley. Arthur Atkinson joined the Hammers after the season had begun. He had been riding a motorbike from boyhood and had experience of grass-track and rough riding before linking up with Blackpool in 1928. Arthur went on to skipper Leeds and became Yorkshire Champion in 1929. Wintering down-under, he made the West Australian title his own and then came back to Britain to join Wembley. He had a bit of a stay with York before joining the happy Hammers where he continued to develop as a rider. In 1936 he became a Test racer and was to be part of two Australian tours.

Blos Blomfield, Tom Lougher and Morian Hansen, the 'Great Dane', were other West Ham debutants. Hansen went to Hackney Wick in 1935. When the Second World War came Hansen, who never wore goggles, joined the RAF and was decorated with the Distinguished Flying Cross and the George Medal. Always a brave rider, he proved to be an equally courageous warrior. With Wilkinson and Croombs starting, West Ham had a good season, making third place in the League. This achievement was in fact quite remarkable as one of the side's top riders, Tiger Stevenson, played no part in the campaign, having been laid low in a road accident. Both Croombs and Wilkinson made the Star Riders' Championship final, Tommy managed third place and as a bonus was selected to ride for England in the Test series, as was Reg Bounds. Wilkinson rode in all five Test matches for Australia.

Arthur Atkinson.

1931 Southern League

Team	PL	W	D	L	Pts
Wembley	38	29	1	8	59
Stamford Bridge	38	27	0	9	54
West Ham	38	23	0	15	46
Crystal Palace	38	22	0	16	44
Wimbledon	38	19	1	18	39
High Beech	38	19	1	18	39
Southampton	38	18	0	20	36
Belle Vue (Res)	38	14	0	24	28
Lea Bridge	38	11	0	27	22
Coventry	38	8	1	29	17

The Southern League was organized by a group of track owners calling themselves the Association of Motorcycle Track Racing Promoters, while the Northern League was controlled by a group called the Northern Dirt-Track Owners Association. These two groups amalgamated in 1932 to form the National Speedway Association.

1931 Northern League

Team	PL	W	D	L	Pts
Belle Vue	18	12	0	6	24
Leeds	18	10	1	7	21
Sheffield	17	10	0	7	20
Leicester	15	8	0	7	16
Preston	16	5	1	10	11
Glasgow	12	2	0	10	4

Only six teams competed in the Northern League in 1931, and for the third time in succession the fixtures were never completed.

Bluey, Miny and Ray

As was his wont, Bluey wintered in his native land after the conclusion of the 1931 season, again doing well on the tracks that had inspired him as a boy. But the 'Bathurst Flyer' met yet more evidence of his wider fame one balmy night in Sydney. An exhibition race pitted Wilkinson against three touring Americans, relative unknowns outside their own state circuits at the time, but who would each make their mark in the sport. There was Miny Waln, who after finishing his speedway education in Australia would become North American Speedway Champion in 1932, Ray Grant, the man that would hold that title in 1933 and a young man with the catchy name of Cordy Milne.

Crystal Palace, London Champions 1931. From left to right: Tom Farndon, Alf Sawford, 'Skid' Pitcher, Joe Francis, Harry Shepherd, F.C. Mockford (managing director), Triss Sharp, Roger Frogley, Nobby Key, Ron Johnson. The man in front with the cup is Harry H. Harold, the Chief Steward.

Before the race there was some joking about more Yanks coming to sort the Wilkinson lad out and as the racers took to the track the local man did look a bit outnumbered. Waln and Grant had built up quite a reputation as a riding partnership while on tour and from the start of the race put Bluey in third spot, Milne seemingly having problems with his mount. After almost a lap, Bluey was still trailing the Americans. However, it was as impossible to get around them as it was to manoeuvre inside them. Waln was holding fast on the inside while Grant covered Wilkinson's way out. The only way through would be to get between Miny and Grant. However, every time Bluey tried it, Grant got in his way. Wilkinson was in no mood to give up in front of his compatriots and pressed on. As the yellow flag dropped he made an almost reckless charge down the straight, smashing between the pair as they catapulted round for the bend, flesh, bone and metal banging and boring. Bluey understood that he could not waver in his resolve to break out; being caught in two minds at that point would result in an unthinkable tangle that promised to take an awful toll on him and/or his opponents. His nerves stayed sure and his control of his machine remained steadfast. Bluey made it through and cut in front of Waln, obliging Grant to follow his line to hang on to second place and continue to chase. Waln was beaten and the powerful pair had been split. 'The Custom House Comet' came home with yards to spare, another American assault thoroughly vanquished. A more perilous example of tactical racing more boldly carried out would be hard to imagine. The spectators jumped to their feet and cheered in admiration. The educated audience knew that they had witnessed a unique sporting performance and a fine example of all that was best in speedway; meticulous preparation, intelligent understanding of tactics, supreme spatial awareness swathed in courage, emanating out of resourceful thinking. Waln and Grant went home thinking that maybe the real high spots of speedway were not destined to be taken by Americans for many years, but Australia and Wilkinson had lit a fire in the belly of the young man who limped home last in that race. The world, its speedways and Bluey Wilkinson had not heard the last of Cordy Milne.

5

HOSKINS, WIZARD OF OZ

Johnnie Hoskins had been managing Wembley when Bluey arrived in London but when Johnnie came to Custom House the two Australians became good friends. Johnnie was a true believer in the power of the media. Everything was newsworthy and he made sure his riders received good write-ups in the press. Few occasions were unworthy of a report for Hoskins. When a rider married, Johnnie made sure they rode round in his famous glass coach and he was very attentive to the supporters' club he did much to create. In West Ham the supporters' group was very large and enthusiastic, and they loved Bluey. In later years Bluey would receive anything up to 1,000 fan letters in a week.

In 1932 Johnnie Hoskins took the trip to Australia with a team of English and Australian riders for a tour of the Commonwealth. There was nothing like a sea trip for a holiday in those days, according to the travel agents, but a trip with over twenty young speedway riders was something of a challenge. There were about a thousand passengers. Hoskins found Wilkinson to often be a lonely, thoughtful travelling companion but always ready to talk about his favourite topic, psychology. Wilkinson wasn't just a cerebral character though and was first to the swimming pool and among the first to start the deck games. He would regularly take a run round the deck and when the ship got into port he was one of the first ashore. On their arrival in Perth the party experienced Bush hunting, horse riding and surfing. Phil Bishop discovered that a horse was like a speedway machine in that it too had no brakes, and being the 'king of crashes' fell off. But unlike a motorbike the horse didn't hang around and he had to walk home. He was later to break three ribs at the fast Royal Showgrounds in Adelaide, which put him out of the tour. Due to his spills, Phil was one of the top attractions in speedway. After a civic reception in Sydney, Wilkinson made his way over the Blue Mountains to his home town of Bathurst. He stayed there for the rest of the tour, commuting to race nights at the Sydney Royale. The team also raced at the Brisbane Royal Showgrounds on a grass track (but Bluey stayed in Bathurst) before returning to England and the new season.

Opposite and above: Phil 'King of the Crash' Bishop.

Right: Jack Parker.

Graham Warren, Birmingham, 1951.

The Royale Road

The Royale at the Royal Agricultural Showgrounds, Moore Park, Sydney, was synonymous with Australian speedway. It was one of the world's great speedway venues, with its fabulous spectator facilities. In its day it was known as the Wembley of the southern hemisphere. Jack Parker believed the track to be the best speedway in the world and all the great riders in the history of the sport had ridden on it. The Royale had a narrow track. With its solid wood (later concrete), safety fence and its potential for high speeds it was considered by some as literally a killer track and it did claim some notables of the sport including Lionel Levy, Geoff Curtis, Barry Hopkin, Rodger Browne, Ken Mapp and Bob Staples. Many riders subsequently refused to race on the track. But there was something fascinating about the Royale for the most skilful and adventurous men. As a stadium, the Royale was built on classic lines. It was not unlike a Roman coliseum. Modern track legend Ivan Mauger once remarked that the place made racers feel like gladiators. It was an egg-shaped circuit around one-third of a mile (557 yards or 509 metres) in length. The 'sharp' end of the egg was at the Pit turn, the southern end and the wider turn was at the northern end between the Members' stand and the Bull Pens. A fast mile race might be covered in 59 to 60 seconds (about 60mph/97kph). In a 1937 programme the promoters claimed that the Royale was the fastest speedway track in the world. Speedway racing was first held at the Royale in 1926 (then The Royal) and continued for seventy years. The last of the regular weekly meetings were staged in the 1980s but the last ever event was held on Saturday 27 July 1996. Many who attended meetings at the Royale will recall the famous three-tier Members' stand on the second turn, at the northern end of the arena. With its huge white clock tower, it had been a landmark from 1924 onwards. The Members' stand could seat 8,000 people and competitors knew that when the top deck of this stand was full on a Saturday night, they would get more prize money, as they shared the gate takings. The equally famous Suttor stand watched over the starting and finishing line. The big, open, concrete Martin and Angus stand was at the southern end of the arena opposite the Members' stand, in between turns three and four of the circuit. It was under this stand that the continuingly vibrating Pits were located. The Sinclair stand was the last of the spectator areas to be built. Constructed in the post-war era, it stood between the Suttor stand and the Martin and Angus stand.

In a 1934 programme the 'Official Electrician' at the Royale stated that it took 25,000 Philips coil type light globes to light up the venue for racing. The wooden safety fence, which had been erected during the reign of Johnnie Hoskins in 1926, acted as a sounding board on that track, seemingly doubling the volume of the roar of the bikes. The Members' stand magnified the noise yet again as the echo of four bikes screaming down the constricted straights at 70mph pulsated through its structure. Every race at the Royale seemed to be a spectacle. There were few riders who were undaunted by the Sydney track. The average speed was 60mph and the corners came up so fast that the riders had to rely on pure instinct to get round them. These turns were sharp and

Ron Johnson in the lead.

Left: West Ham's Eric Chitty.

Right: Jimmy Gibb.

the crowd intimidating. Nevertheless, the circuit fascinated many better riders in the way that danger intrigues the courageous. Bluey once said it was the only track that scared him but he loved the experience of competing on it. Graham Warren once commented that the Royale was big, fast and quite dangerous in that the banking allowed riders to hold the throttle open the whole time. He remarked, 'You don't think of it when you're young, but there was no room for error with those concrete crash walls.' Looking back, Ivan Mauger recollected, 'With those high stands so close to the track, the crowd was almost on top of you. When the stadium was packed the atmosphere was tremendous.'

There were aspects of the Royale that remained almost unchanged throughout its history, giving one the sense that one was travelling back in time on entering the great old edifice. The huge yellow water truck on the well-cared-for the centre green, the Royal Agricultural Show officials in their white coats that ended just above their boots and the worn and crinkled recording of *God Save The Queen* that was churned out before competition commenced. But the Grand Old Lady of speedway finally dipped under the waves of sporting history. The 90mph black ribbon had been the stage upon which the skill and daring of speedway had been played out for over seventy years. Rod McDonald won the final race at the Royale in front of nearly 30,000 people.

Keeping Tabs on the Wounded Tiger

In 1932, West Ham took part in the National Speedway Association Trophy, which was a League-style competition the successor of which would be the National League Championship. The National Trophy was the product of a fusion between the Northern and Southern Leagues. The West Ham team at this time was the basis of the side that would ride at Custom House for the next seven years. Ed 'Flash' Barker, a former wrestler and Eric Chitty, a fair-haired Canadian who had a fine singing voice and would often serenade the massed support West Ham commanded, were introduced into the side as was another Canadian export, Jimmy Gibb. Captain Tiger Stevenson rode for several weeks with a broken collarbone, an injury he picked up at the start of the 1932 campaign following a fall. The injury was only discovered after he collapsed during a meeting a few weeks after the accident. In the much tougher League, the Hammers managed to hold on to sixth place; the Lions of Wembley were streets ahead. Wilkinson and Croombs were again the main point takers of the side. Croombs continued his custom of making the Star Riders Championship final and won the prestigious 'Cundy' Trophy.

The 1932 season saw the replacing of the Southern and Northern Speedway Leagues, with the first running of the National League.

1932 National League

Team	PL	W	D	L	Pts
Wembley	16	13	0	3	26
Crystal Palace	16	11	1	4	23
Belle Vue	16	9	1	6	19
Stamford bridge	16	8	1	7	17
Wimbledon	16	8	1	7	17
West Ham	16	7	0	9	14
Coventry	16	6	0	10	8
Clapton	16	4	0	12	8
Plymouth	16	4	0	12	8

With the North and South now combining for the single National League, Johnnie Hoskins' Lions also took the National Trophy and the London Cup trophy. With the institution of a supporters club and an end-of-season membership of nearly 20,000, things looked very good for the Empire Stadium management.

Know what it means to work hard on machines – it's a labour of love...

As the mid-1930s approached, Bluey was making something in excess of £2,000 a year, but he had earned every last penny. He had to fight his way up in an environment where the big riders got too much money and the lesser lights could only pick up what was left. The best motors went to the men with the names, and the beginners took what they could get. Many talented lads fell by the wayside for no other reason than the loss of heart in what must have felt like, and to some extent was, a closed shop. However, Bluey, along with a few others, had the tenacity and warrior quality that not only breaks through but prevails overall.

Success brought its own problems. Bluey might be involved in four or five meetings a week, commuting the length and breadth of the realm, from Glasgow to Plymouth, from Cardiff to King's Oak. Often Bluey's fellow Hammers Tommy Croombs and Tiger Stevenson would be at the same events. Mostly they got paid but sometimes a track would fold up and they got nothing. If there was any dispute over prize money they stood together. On those occasions Tiger Stevenson was invariably the spokesman for the trio. Diplomatic but firm and persistent, Stevenson was an imposing man. For all that, it was not unusual for the riders to be paid with money straight from the turnstiles and walk away with their pockets bulging with 'the Kings Copper'. After a time a number of organizations did start to book riders on a percentage of booking fees and this worked for a while but riders outside the top bracket were massively exploited and the sport gave every sign of disintegrating. Although an extremely successful rider, Wilkinson was no stranger to disappointment. The formative years of his career were full of 'runner-up' experiences, having to bend the knee to riders such as Vic Huxley and the British Individual Championship eluded him. Once he was picked to ride for a Dominion side and on the day of the match his place was given to Jack Chapman. This said, he made each reversal his education and his extraordinary popularity was founded on the public's consciousness of this. As the massed spectators of speedway across Britain witnessed his improvement, he became a popular personality within the sport and beyond. He went from being the underdog to the man to beat in the space of a few years in the early to mid-1930s. His reputation as the hard-worker who succeeded was the quality British followers of the sport admired and the East Enders who packed Custom House Stadium loved. 'Bluey never gives up' became a Cockney mantra and he never did. Relatively few of us realize our dreams; those of us that might will recognize the 'way of Wilkinson'.

6

TESTING TIMES

The First Test

The arrangements for the first ever official England *v.* Australia Test match were made difficult as a result of the rivalry between the various speedway promoters. Wimbledon Speedway had its headquarters in Fleet Street at the time, which was the centre of the British newspaper industry. As such, the Wimbledon staff were drenched in the press interest in the coming Australian tour. Over the Bank Holiday weekend of 28 May 1930 the Australian Cricket Team, led by Don Bradman, were playing England at Lords. This prompted Wimbledon to suggest that a speedway Test match, staged in London on the evening of 28 May, would benefit commercially from association with the established cricket Test. On the promise that the Wimbledon Test would be only the first of a series, the other promotions agreed to the booking of their star riders and, as the time drew near, various publicity stunts were put in place to ensure that there would be a good turnout for the match itself. There had already been a speedway contest between the two countries. The first solo competition between Australia and England took place at West Ham in 1929. The Australian side for this first match was captain Vic Huxley, Buzz Hibbard, Frank Arthur, Max Grosskreutz, Bill Lamont and Hilary Buchman/Hilary Buchann, who came to England in 1928 to became popular at Wimbledon, White City, Harringay and other International Speedways promotions. He took well to the smaller English tracks and was successful in many Handicap races.

On the evening of 28 May there were long queues at the Wimbledon turnstiles. Admission charges were 1s 2d, 2s 4d and 5s. In the programme (which would have cost you 6d) it was announced: *The Australian Team has been approved by the Australian Authorities who recognise this Event as the First Official Speedway Test Match* – take that West Ham! Newspapers had run stories and posters were put up all over London. As the match was ready to start the traffic around the stadium was chaotic and the start of the series had to be delayed for forty-five minutes in order to get everyone through the turnstiles. The riders finally lined up with their machines for the formal presentations in front of 30,000 fans. The English team wore white jerseys with a red lion emblazoned on the back and the Australians were in red with their traditional symbol of a kangaroo. The England side were Jim Kempster (captain) (Wimbledon), Wal Phillips

Above: The Kangaroos of 1930. Billy Lamont (far left) is not amused.

Opposite: Max Grosskreutz.

(Stamford Bridge), Jack Parker (Coventry), Frank Varey (Belle Vue), Jack Ormston (Wembley), Roger Frogley (Crystal Palace) and Gus Kuhn (Stamford Bridge) as reserve. The Australians fielded Vic Huxley (captain) (Harringay), Frank Arthur (Stamford Bridge), Max Grosskreutz (Belle Vue), Dick Case (Wimbledon), Billy Lamont (Wimbledon), Ron Johnson (Crystal Palace) and Arnie Hansen (Southampton) as reserve. Some days before the first official Test, Frank Arthur was unfit after falling at Stamford Bridge but he struggled in to Plough Lane to give an excellent performance. Jack Parker was also one of the 'walking wounded', coming back after a number of spills.

The first match consisted of just nine heats and Vic Huxley led the way for Australia by being unbeaten in any of his three rides. In the first heat he lowered the Wimbledon track record. It wasn't to be one of the longest standing of times as Billy Lamont set a new standard in heat 7. He went on to become the first racer to ride a maximum in an England *v.* Australia Test match. Roger Frogley top scored for England with six points and Kempster managed five. Australia humbled England 17-35.

Above: Ron Johnson falling during a 1930
Test series.

Right: Hard man Ron Johnson, New Cross,
and of course the girls!

Opposite: Dickie Case.

Opposite page
Above left: Where there's a wheel … Ron Johnson.

Above right: The dapper Ron Johnson.

Below: From left to right: Ron Johnson, Max Grosskreutz and Roarin' Johnnie Hoskins at Odsal.

This page
Right: Ron Johnson, Australian enigma.

Below: Gus Kuhn, Wimbledon, October 1935.

Toss-up at Crystal Palace, Engand *v.* Australia Test match, 1931. Colin Watson of England (right) and Vic Huxley of Australia (left) watch promoter Fred Mockford do the honours. Other riders in the picture are Len Woods (Australia) and Jack Ormston (England).

Australian Scorers:

Vic Huxley	9
Frank Arthur	6
Max Grosskreutz	6
Billy Lamont	6
Ron Johnson	5
Dick Case	3
Arnie Hansen (Res)	Did not race

English Scorers:

Roger Frogley	6
Jim Kempster	5
Wal Phillips	4
Jack Parker	1
Jack Ormston	1
Frank Varey	0 (two rides)
Gus Kuhn	0 (from one ride)

All the riders rode three times unless otherwise indicated.

Australian riders won seven of the nine heats. Huxley won three, Arthur had two victories and Max Grosskreutz and Lamont had one a piece. Two English riders won a heat, Jim Kempster and Roger Frogley.

As there were just the nine heats during the second half of the evening, a series of contests were held to find the 'Champion of the Meeting'. This involved a competition between the Aussie riders and another consisting of Poms only. The winner of each pool would ride off to establish a victor:

Aussie Pool results:

Huxley beat Case

Johnson beat Arthur

Lamont beat Grosskreutz

The three-rider decider saw Huxley come in first from Johnson and Lamont.

Pom Pool results:

Kempster beat Frogley

Phillips beat Varey

The other two English riders declined to race.

Kempster beat Phillips and so met Huxley for the title. Although the English skipper was also captain of the Wimbledon team, whose track was being used for the Test, the crowd knew he had a mountain to climb to beat Hux in the form he had hit on the evening. Huxley did win at a canter, walking away from Plough Lane undefeated. The reserves also had a competition which resulted in Hansen's defeat at the hands of Kuhn.

Australia had won the first ever speedway Test match. This could never be taken away from them but the home side went on to win the next four encounters at Belle Vue (twice), Stamford Bridge and Wembley. These matches had 16 heats and eight riders with two reserves. The number of heats continued to be inconsistent in future years with 12, 15 and 18-heat formulas being used. A combined total of over 150,000 people watched the confrontations of 1930.

Recognition of his growing reputation and skill came when Bluey was chosen as reserve for the third England *v.* Australia Test match in 1930. He didn't manage to score a point but he was back for the fifth Test and managed to grab a couple of points for his side.

Bound for Australia

In following years Tests were held at Crystal Palace, Leicester, New Cross, Harringay and West Ham. In September 1932, in the midst of the depression, a massive crowd of 82,000 were at Wembley to see England win 51-42. Although they invariably came close, the Australians did not manage to win the Ashes until 1934. At the end of that year the first official English Lions touring party sailed for the antipodes. The first official Test match between England and Australia, outside of England, was held at the Royale,

Above: Joe Abbott.

Left: Wally Little.

Dusty Haigh.

Sydney, on Saturday 15 December 1934. It was the twenty-sixth Test match between the two countries and it drew over 50,000 spectators and many hung themselves, riskily, over the wooden safety fence during the races. From close quarters they waved their programmes and absorbed the exhilarating sight of their heroes and the deafening noise from their machines.

The Australia v England Test Match 1934

Results

Heat 1	Grosskreutz, Stevenson, Little	63.2	new track record
Heat 2	Van Praag, Mitchell, Langton	65.0	
Heat 3	Wilkinson, Case, Abbott	64.8	
Heat 4	Stevenson, Van Praag, Mitchell	64.8	
Heat 5	Wilkinson, Case, Langton	66.0	
Heat 6	Grosskreutz, Abbott, Little	64.4	
Heat 7	Stevenson, Case, Wilkinson	65.6	Haigh for Parkinson
Heat 8	Langton, Grosskreutz, Phillips	65.4	
Heat 9	Van Praag, Varey, Mitchell	66.2	

Australia won 35-19

Australia					England				
Max Grosskreutz (Cap)	3	3	2	8	Tiger Stevenson (Cap)	2	3	3	8
Wally Little	1	1	–	2	Cliff Parkinson	–	–	*	0
Lionel Van Praag	3	2	3	8	Eric Langton	1	1	3	5
Clem Mitchell	2	1	1	4	Wal Phillips	–	–	1	1
Dick Case	2	2	2	6	Frank Varey	–	–	2	2
Bluey Wilkinson	3	3	1	7	Joe Abbott	1	2	–	3
Dick Sulway (Res.)		DNR			Dusty Haigh	–	*	*	0

The third match of that year's Test series came to Belle Vue on 6 July 1935. The Australians had lost the first two matches and so this represented their last chance to keep the event alive. The team that faced the English was indeed formidable: Dicky Case and Mick Murphy (res) of Hackney Wick, the Wimbledon men Jack Sharpe and Vic Huxley, who captained the side, Lionel Van Praag, the pride of the Wembley Lions and West Ham's Bluey Wilkinson. Ron Johnson of New Cross, who dropped just 5 of the 18 points available to him during the match, completed the line-up. But England, managed by Alex Jackson, got their revenge for the previous year. In front of a record crowd they took the match 59-48. In front of his own supporters the England skipper Eric Langton won 17 points, making him the top scorer of the encounter. The rest of the side included Jack Parker of Harringay, Tommy Croombs and Tiger Stevenson from West Ham, New Cross superstar Tom Farndon, and riding on their home track Joe Abbot, Bill Kitchen and Bob Harrison.

The final Australia *v.* England Test match held at the Royale took place on 1 January 1994 in front of a crowd of 17,000. Australia won 68-40. The teams that day were as follows

England	Australia
Steve Schofield	Tony Langdon
Paul Thorpe	Stephen Davies
Joe Screen (captain)	Leigh Adams (captain)
Andy Smith	Jason Crump
David Norris	Jason Lyons
Sean Wilson	Craig Boyce
Ben Howe	Mick Poole

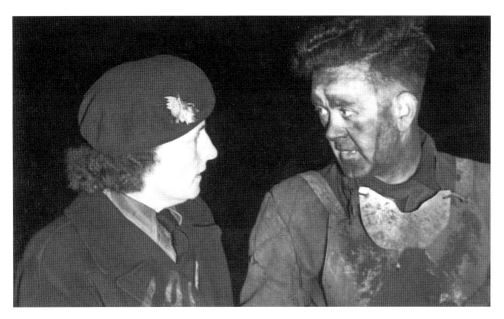

Above: Alice Hart and Belle Vue skipper Eric Langton.

Below: Bill Kitchen (centre) with friends at Wembley.

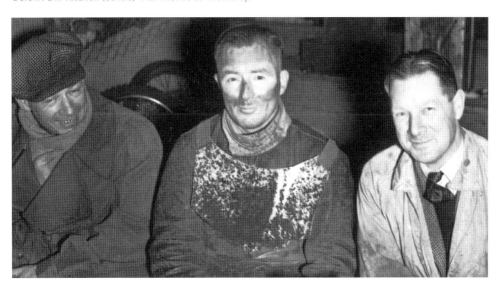

Results

England

Sean Wilson	2	m	1	r	3	1	7
David Norris	–	1	–	*	–	*	1
Joe Screen (Capt)	2	2	–	1	r	1	6
Steve Schofield	3	–	1	3	2	2	11
Andy Smith	–	-	*	–	–	*	0
Paul Thorp	2	1	1	1	2	3	10
Ben Howe (Res)	3	2	–	–	*	*	5

Australia

Leigh Adams(Capt)	3	3	3	3	3	f	15
Tony Langdon	1	2	2	1	1	3	10
Jason Lyons	–	2	2	–	2	–	7
Jason Crump	1	3	–	2	1	2	9
Craig Boyce	3	3	2	2	3	2	15
Mick Poole	1	1	3	3	1	3	12
Stephen Davies (Res)	DNR						

Other Australian Test match venues were to include the Melbourne Motordrome, Olympic Park and the smaller, but historic, Sydney Sports Ground, which was situated on the corner of Driver Avenue. The Sydney Football Stadium and its car park were built on the site after it closed on 25 March 1955. Bluey Wilkinson won the 1938 New South Wales Title at the Sports Ground just after he won the World Championship against such riders as Lionel Van Praag, Norman and Jack Parker, Bob Harrison, Aub Lawson, Jack Milne, Wilbur Lamoreax, Arthur Atkinson and Geoff Pymar. Bluey had won the New South Wales Championship first in 1935 and won it again in 1939.

Bluey the Aussie

From the first series until his retirement from the track in 1939, Bluey Wilkinson was always to be part of the Australian Test team. In his Test career he amassed 540 points, making him the best ever Australian rider. His nearest rival was Max Grosskreutz with 497 points. Bluey appeared in all the Test matches of 1932. There were 45,000 at the Stamford Bridge Test early in June of that year. This is perhaps not surprising given the support for speedway at the time as well as the talent on show. For instance, Bluey had to face the likes of Jack Parker, Eric Langton, Tom Farndon and Frank Varey.

Wilkinson had some formidable characters on his side. Some of the most awesome were Vic Huxley, Ron Johnson, Frank Arthur and Lionel Van Praag, who began his speedway career in 1926 and rode for his country from 1931. He was skipper with the Wembley side but he did not reach his peak until 1936, when numerous successes culminated in his victory in the first World Speedway Championship. However, Van Praag started working life as a typewriter mechanic but he developed his engineering prowess to become one of the finest engineers around the speedways.

Syd Jackson, Wimbledon, July 1935.

Above: Running repairs for Ron Johnson.

Left: Squib Burton.

Below: Ron Johnson out in front.

George Newton (left) shakes hands
with Eric Langton.

In the first part of the 1930s Bluey Wilkinson had established himself as one of the most powerful Test riders available to the Australians and, still a young man, promised even more for the future. By 1933 the top five Australian scorers in Test matches against England were as follows:

The Top Five Australian Test Scorers 1930-1933

Rider	1930					1931					1932					1933				
	1	2	3	4	5	1	2	3	4	5	1	2	3	4	5	1	2	3	4	5
Vic Huxley	9	7	11	12	12	6	6	1	10	10	5	9	6	9	12	12	16	8½	12	13
Dick Case	3	4	5	7	3	6	8	–	–	–	6	12	10	10	5	8	12	15	10	12
Max Grosskreutz	6	12	7	5	4	7	4	6	9	7	7	7	4	5	2	0	9	13	18	4
Bluey Wilkinson	–	–	0	–	2	4	3	5	8	4	5	9	6	6	3	8	16	14	14	16
Frank Arthur	6	6	8	6	–	9	7	11	6	8	6	8	5	5	2	–	–	–	–	–

There were nineteen Australian riders used over the four years. Their scores are ranked below:

Rider	Points	Rider	Points
Vic Huxley	186.5	Charlie Spinks	19
Dick Case	136	Dick Smythe	17
Max Grosskreutz	129	Ernie Evans	16
Bluey Wilkinson	123	Arnie Hansen	6
Frank Arthur	93	Bobby Blake	5
Ron Johnson	75	Dick Wise	4
Billy Lamont	55	Col. Stewart	3
Lionel Van Praag	40	Jack Sharp	3
Jack Chapman	33	Len Woods	3
		Bruce McCallum	2
		Total	**948.5**

The top ten English riders, Jack Parker, Ginger Lees, Eric Langton, Frank Varey, Tiger Stevenson, Tom Farndon, Wal Phillips, Squib Burton, Syd Jackson and Colin Watson scored a total of 759 points. However, the Australian top ten scorers totalled 899.5 points. This indicates that while England was stronger in depth, the Australians had the more powerful individual riders. This is confirmed by looking at the top five Test scorers over this period, England *v.* Australia inclusive:

Rider/Nation	Points
Vic Huxley – Australia	186.5
Dick Case – Australia	136
Max Grosskreutz – Australia	129
Jack Parker – England	124
Bluey Wilkinson – Australia	124
Ginger Lees – England	123

The above would constitute the best overall side chosen on Test form from the combined scores of Australian and English riders between 1930 and 1933 (the reserves would have been Frank Varey of England and Frank Arthur of Australia).

Over the first four years of official Test matches, England won 14 and Australia won 6. England scored a total of 1047.5 points, 99 points ahead of Australia. On average the sides were separated by under 5 points in each match.

In 1933 Wimbledon Stadium were asked for the first time since their staging of the very first Test to host another England *v.* Australia match. Once again, in front of 25,000 excited fans Australia triumphed, but this time only by 2 points. At one stage it looked in the bag for the Lions, as after heat 13 they led the Aussies by 11 points, but Australia, inspired by a magnificent 18 points from Max Grosskreutz and double-figure scores from Bluey Wilkinson, Huxley and Case, took the lead in heat 15 and never looked back. Best for the Lions was Ginger Lees with 17. But England took the series yet again.

1934, Australia's series-winning year, was probably Bluey Wilkinson's best as a Test rider and the match at the Empire Stadium, Wembley was one of Bluey's finest displays on the international stage. He was top point scorer with 16 points, followed closely by Max Grosskreutz with 15 points. The captain of that Australian side was Ron Johnson, who was in agony throughout the night from an injury he had received at a meeting earlier in the week. By heat 15, the scores were even at 45 points. At this stage the match could go either way but, in order to win, the English had to beat Johnson, Wilkinson and Grosskreutz in the final three races. Johnson easily won the first. In the next race, England still had an outside chance if the English captain Eric Langton could beat Bluey. But Wilkinson made sure the race went to Australia, timing his run well for a comfortable win. It was all over and Bluey had made sure of his side's victory. Max Grosskreutz tied the whole series up with a comfortable win over the demoralized English in the final race. The groundwork on a series win had been established in the very bastion of English speedway.

Top-man Bluey

The pre-war tests were, as crowd pullers, phenomenal events. As sporting epics they were worthy of the great rivalry between Poms and Aussies in the field of physical endeavour. Bluey scored 181 points in 23 pre-war matches for Australia against England and was the first ever Test rider to score maximum points in every match in a Test series during the 1937-38 five-match Test series held in Sydney. It was to remain an unbeaten record.

Note: The foregoing tables refer to riders' performances in all the speedway Tests, including those of reserves, when they were called upon. The first Test in 1930 was contested over nine heats by teams of six with one reserve, the scoring being 3, 2, and 1 point for first, second and third place respectively. The remaining 1930 matches, as well as the 1931 and 1932 series, were between eight-a-side teams with two reserves. There were 16 heats to a match, but the scoring remained the same. In 1933 the scoring was altered to 4, 2, and 1 point for the heat placings, and matches were lengthened to 18 races. Teams, however, were cut down to six a side, though two reserves were still allowed. There was a reversion to a 3, 2, and 1 point scoring system for the 1934 Tests.

7

ROUND AND ROUND, DOWN AND UP

By the start of the 1933 season it was clear that the popularity of speedway was in decline. For supporters the most frustrating aspect of the sport was the number of false starts. The coming of the starting gate was, as such, a real boost for the tracks. As is nearly always the case, necessity is the mother of invention, but West Ham needed something else. The side had some good riders but major silverware was conspicuous by its absence. At the mighty West Ham Stadium the Hammers looked invulnerable but away from their own dirt, as a team, they appeared to be a shambles. Defeat is an epidemic. It floors a team like a virus. The mechanics received a bonus of ten shillings each when the team won, but loss brought only pain.

However, there were still some marvellous individual performances, in particular from Bluey. On an individual level he was beginning to make success a habit but his reputation made those he competed against more alert to his skills and more ready to work together to beat him. For all this, he was the inspiration of the Australian Test sides of the 1930s. In a match with Bristol he once more came into contact with Cordy Milne, who by 1933 was the kingpin of that side. Both Croombs and Wilkinson were wary of the American and from the start worked together to block his way to the front. But Milne was a racer who wasn't going to take this kind of treatment lying down. He fought like a cougar for a way through, but each time he was foiled by one or other of the West Ham pair. Partly in frustration and partly in desperation, Cordy battered away at the moving wall in front of him. Hitting more than 60mph on the straights, he attempted to get round Wilkinson but had to draw back as the fence threatened to eat him. Then he made for what looked like a gap left by Croombs, close to the line, only to see Tommy snatch away his hope. The rush into the final turn was the do-or-die moment. Milne rammed in, threatening the Hammers with his rumbling will and all the guts in his machine. With the finish running in at them, the trio were slammed together, linked in battle and metal. It was a screaming, frenzy of a finish. But it was Bristol and Cordy who took the race having breached the claret and blue barrier with only feet left to race.

It seemed the spirit of West Ham had taken umbrage at this defeat when Cordy Milne's brother Jack lost a thumb at Custom House, but a month later he was back competing. Such injuries were an occupational hazard and even Bluey Wilkinson was not immune. While racing he was hit in the face by a razor-like stone shot from a whirring back wheel. Bluey looked as if he'd asked a member of the West Ham hatchet boys for the last dance at Stratford Palais. The wound had sucked in a fistful of cinders. This was to leave him with the blue, tattoo-like mark that so many coal miners would be familiar with.

Wilkinson never liked to lose. He hated it. But rather than concoct excuses he would seek reasons. For him excuses were the whining of the weak. He had an almost scientific approach, seeking wisdom from setbacks rather than recrimination. He could deconstruct races and imagine alternative outcomes. Wilkinson could use his losses, analyse and learn from them and then make himself concentrate on the next race and apply his new insight. He listened to what everyone had to say, paying attention to boasts, grumbling and every observation. He considered the tiniest detail and then made up his own mind what to do and perhaps more importantly, how to do it and when. You only had to watch him race to understand the advantage this gave him. Following a sluggish start he would not ease off. He didn't let knocks and bruises put him out of competition. He was an avid reader, developing his knowledge of psychology and in particular the concept of willpower. He was heard to have debates on Christian Science in the pits and loved to read and talk about classic literature. He derived a great deal of inspiration from works like *Moby Dick* and *The Last of the Mohicans*. He was also a fan of Shakespeare and once remarked how the Globe Theatre looked like a 'wall-of-death'!

Hello Ron, Goodbye Ron

Another star individual of the West Ham side in 1933 was Tiger Stevenson. With Wilkinson and Croombs he helped pull the Hammers out of their slough and the side ended the season with a respectable spot in the League, just a point behind Wimbledon. Stevenson's fine season was confirmed by his nomination to race against Ron Johnson of Crystal Palace for the British Match Race Championship. The Aussie-Scot was a tough draw for Stevenson. He had been a good amateur boxer and continued to compete on the track even after losing toes and fingers. The following year he was to make the highest score in the Test series riding for his adopted country. But Stevenson was in frightening form and the West Ham rider won both legs of the Championship to become one of the select band of Londoners to make star class. Appreciation of Stevenson's exploits was shown when he was awarded the captaincy of England for four of that year's Test matches. The final match of the Test series at Custom House attracted 82,400, although it is likely to have been 100,000 as West Ham always had more than its share of 'gatecrashers'. The stadium was so huge that it was almost impossible to police, especially as there seemed to be hundreds of informal ways in, from calling in favours from relatives to climbing over the back of the stands. Bluey was again in the Kangaroos side, as he had been for the whole series. He was Australia's top scorer, churning out double figures in four matches. But the Tiger led his nation to a 3-2 series win. He too notched up double figures in every match he appeared in. Stevenson was never to have a better year in speedway.

Tommy Croombs got to the Star Riders' final, as did Bluey, by way of a run-off that included Tom Farndon and Tiger Stevenson's adversary in the British Championship, Ron Johnson. From the off Tom and Bluey had a real dust-up but the engagement was cut short when Wilkinson's front tyre wobbled and faltered. Farndon shot past him as did Johnson, leaving the unhappy Hammer to limp home third.

1933 National League

Team	PL	W	D	L	Pts
Belle Vue	36	31	0	5	62
Wimbledon	36	23	0	13	46
West Ham	36	21	3	12	45
Crystal Palace	36	21	0	15	42
Clapton	36	19	3	14	41
Wembley	36	19	1	16	39
Coventry	36	10	2	24	22
Sheffield	36	11	0	25	22
Plymouth	36	11	0	25	22
Nottingham	36	9	1	26	19

This season saw the start of the Belle Vue domination of speedway. They won the League easily and also took the National Trophy. They remained winners until 1937 when West Ham ended their reign, though they went on to win the National Trophy for five consecutive seasons.

In the close season Crystal Palace was closed down and the whole team moved across to New Cross.

As the attendance figures dropped, King's Oak in Essex and the Stamford Bridge circuit in London closed.

The tapes-start mechanism was introduced in 1933 and the technology of the apparatus has changed little over the years.

Rolling on

West Ham fielded a side in the Reserve League in 1934. It was also referred to as the Second Division of the National League. As such, if you didn't know much about speedway you might have thought the Hammers were sending at least four teams into the fray!

Stevenson, Wilkinson and Croombs all continued to show the same form as the previous season. Arthur Atkinson, Eric Gregory, Arthur Warwick and Broncho Dixon were also holding their own. Tiger would be top man at Custom House that year, just beating Bluey for the distinction of being top scorer. Tommy Croombs wasn't too far behind Wilkinson but the competition had been fierce and West Ham didn't do badly to make fourth place when their match schedule was completed. The defeat of

Broncho Dixon, West Ham.

Wembley in the semi-final of the London Cup brought hope that some substantial silverware would at last find its way to the East End. The match could have gone any way at the end and with Stevenson, West Ham's top rider and captain, out injured, Stan Dell was drafted into the team from the reserve side as a replacement for the crocked skipper. In the first leg at New Cross Stan rode above himself and scored 10 paid 11 from six rides. Unfortunately New Cross were too strong for the fighting Hammers in the final. West Ham also reached the ACU Cup final at Plough Lane but Belle Vue added to their honours by beating the Hammers 56-51. There was some consolation for the West Ham supporters as the Custom House boys ran away with the Junior League, not losing one match in their season. The West Ham side included Ken Brett, Rol Stobart, Stan Dell and Wal Morton.

Stan Dell, Birmingham captain and England international.

1934 National League

Team	PL	W	D	L	Pts
Belle Vue	32	27	0	5	54
Wembley	32	26	0	6	52
New Cross	32	21	0	11	42
West Ham	32	16	1	15	33
Wimbledon	32	16	0	16	32
Harringay	32	14	1	17	29
Birmingham	32	9	0	23	18
Plymouth	32	8	2	18	18
Walthamstow	32	5	0	27	10

The Star Riders' final was again graced by Bluey Wilkinson and Tommy Croombs, although neither West Ham rider made the run-off. The Match Race title left the custody of Tiger Stevenson to sit on Vic Huxley's mantlepiece at the start of the season, but the Hammers' leader was to be selected for three England Test match sides in 1934. Tommy Croombs was also given three caps during the series. As seemed to be the custom, Wilkinson was ever-present in the Australian team for the duration of the Test season. He reached double figures on two occasions and was top point winner; he got 16 in the final Test at Custom House.

8

THE MACHINE

The speedway motorcycle that started off as no more than a stripped-down road bike was, by the mid-1930s, a specialist machine, turned out by hand with consideration and many hours of skilled labour. This meant that the demand for these motors far exceeded the supply. Money was not the only factor. The riders with proven ability and big names had the first choice of all equipment. Those further down the food chain found that they were severely restricted by their relatively stock machines. As such they were obliged to come to some arrangement with the leading riders to provide them with a share of prize money in return for use and maintenance of the better bikes. If a renting rider got injured, the motor was simply hired to someone else. Some riders, like Sprouts Elder, who was to retire to become a California Highway Patrolman in 1935, might have as many as six riders racing for them and make a good deal of money as a consequence. It was a very severe form of capitalism, a renter having control over a rider's means of life and labour and raking off surplus value; it was in fact blatant exploitation. However, it was legitimate business and the more astute riders won enough on these good machines to be able to demand better equipment and to buy good motors themselves.

Bluey Wilkinson wasn't part of this. He got information from tuners and from good riders. For most of his career he looked after his own motors. Jack Harris, one of the top and most highly paid mechanics, saw the tuning of a racing motor as a task that demanded patience, care and cleanliness. For him, if one followed that dictum, anyone was capable of such work. A speedway rider could only go so far on the merits of his skill and riding technique; his machine would always enhance or limit these qualities. Almost from the start of speedway, the track machine departed from its road-bound ancestor. Lights, mirrors, gears and brakes were almost immediately abandoned. The tuning of the bike had to be done beforehand as once the race had started the rider could only steer the machine, control the throttle, or pull in the clutch to interrupt the drive of the motor. It was the tuning of the motor that was crucial. A number of factors had to taken into consideration well before any event; the track, its condition, type and length, the weather, the rider, his height, style and weight. The old belt-driven Douglas machines that Bluey rode at the start of his racing career, had been produced from

1907 to 1925, so that when Bluey first rode onto the track it was on a machine which was no longer in production and had been superseded by the more advanced chain-driven bikes. He got hold of a later-model Douglas for his record-breaking races at Bathurst and when he came to Britain he brought a Douglas machine with him. Early on in the 1930s the Australian Test team switched to JAP machines. They won the Ashes from the English in 1934. Bluey was also riding a JAP when he won the World Championship and his effigy displayed in Madam Tussaud's was mounted on a JAP. The JAP was a British bike produced by J.A. Priestwick. It differed from the Douglas in that it had a vertical engine, so the bike was shorter and required a completely different riding technique. It had a 497cc engine, weighed 63 pounds and methanol was used to fuel the bike. The engine had two push rods which operated a two-valve, four-stroke engine – the four strokes being induction, compression, power and exhaust. There were two chains; the primary chain running from the engine to the counter clutch and the secondary chain linking the counter shaft to the rear wheel. The JAP didn't have a battery – a magneto, which was a rotating magnet, was used instead. The magneto ignited the fuel mixture with a high-tension spark. The two valves were the inlet valve, to introduce the fuel mixture and the exhaust valve to remove the burnt gases. Fine tuning was critical because the lift angle of the camshaft affected the amount of air and fuel which could enter the carburettor; more fuel mixture meant more speed. Expert tuning was necessary due to the design of the cylinder head. The even burning of the gases across the top of the piston produced the power to drive the engine. The power came from the cylinder head design and the porting as well as the camshaft and the carburation. In the engines that Bluey was using, these were in the lower section of the engine. Nowadays the engines have overhead camshafts, which provide much more power in a shorter space of time.

The other important area of adjustment was in the compression ratio. The condition of the track could determine the compression ratio. If the track was slick, by adding compression shims under the cylinder barrel the volume of the cylinder would increase and so decrease the compression ratio. If the track was deep, which most were in Bluey's racing days as cinders were used on the track surface, the compression ratio aimed for was around 13.425:1 and up to 15:1. This would be achieved by adding the swept volume to the clearance volume and dividing the total by the clearance volume:

$$\frac{S.V. + C.V.}{C.V.} \quad \frac{497cc + 40}{40} \quad = \quad 13.425$$

If the rider had misjudged the conditions of the track and had allowed for a compression ratio of 13.425 or 15:1, only to find that the track was slick and slippery, he would probably be left at the gate with his wheels spinning and going nowhere fast.

Another decisive variable was the length of the track. Most tracks in those days were a quarter of a mile with a straight stretch bending to an oval shape then another bend leading to a back straight before rounding to the finishing post, but there was any range of exceptions. Not all ovals were the same. They differed in length, the shortest being much shorter than the longest. Some had long straights with tight bends, others had

The Custom House Comet (third from left) in 'civvies'.

broad, sweeping turns connected by relatively short runways. Every time a rider raced, he had to think about the circuit he was to traverse. This, with differences in weather conditions or a slight alteration in surface make up, might mean that he was going to negotiate a track quite unlike the one he had run on the last time he was at the same stadium in Exeter, Glasgow or Custom House.

As speedway bikes had no gearboxes, the length of the straight determined the alterations to be made to the gear ratio. The ideal would be to reach maximum speed when the rider reached the end of the straights. The gear ratio was altered by changing the sprockets on the rear wheel and on the engine. Most riders would have a gear ratio calculator which would quickly show the conversion of sprocket size to gear ratio and of gear ratio to RPM (revolutions per minute) to speed. When Bluey won the World Championship in 1938 he was doing the quarter mile in around 76 to 77 seconds, racing on a cinder track. By the late twentieth century the time had been reduced to between 71 and 72 seconds but the shale tracks that replaced cinder ovals produced a smoother riding surface, so engines were changed to facilitate an overhead camshaft which meant that greater speeds could be achieved more swiftly.

The introduction of the gate was a revolution for the riders of Wilkinson's era. Before this innovation riders made a running start. The coming of the gate meant that the racer had to begin from a standing position. The riders lined up between steel posts. A tape was stretched across in front of the riders, which was controlled by an electric solenoid which was operated by the starter. When the starter broke the contact the tapes flew up above the riders who would, if everything went according to plan, power forward into the race. Because of the standing start, the fine tuning of the engine became even more crucial as speed had to be achieved as quickly as possible.

The story of the speedway can be told through the machine. Riders and mechanics, often the same person in the early days, built and adapted their racers to the context they were competing in; the sport grew out of these mechanisms but these motorbikes were, at the same time, products of the game. This is why speedway is very much a tale of the twentieth century. It is the summation of man and machine, a chronicle of the human development of and interaction with internal combustion.

9

SO NEAR, YET...

The 1935 season was not too old when a revolution came to Custom House, one by the name of Johnnie Hoskins, the self-proclaimed founder of the speedway and certainly the first larger-than-life entrepreneur of sport. He was to change the concept of speedway radically. The sport had already become a business and Hoskins was to do more than anyone else to redefine it as a form of entertainment. Bluey Wilkinson had developed into a semi-leg trailer who put his foot forward coming into a bend and trailed it coming out. He had heavily padded shoulders on his leathers and was unmistakable when on the track. He was becoming a feared and respected racer by 1935 but his strong point was still his spirit, tenacity and resolve. He had become a hardened, skilled, professional rider with a bit more speed than most. Nevertheless, the likes of Huxley, Grosskreutz, Jack Parker, Ron Johnston and Jack Milne were still a match for him in terms of speed and were technically better riders. But given the right conditions and some good fortune at the first bend Wilkinson was often able to time his actions just a split second to the good, or his fast, searching brain would track a line through, or discover an extra metre. One thing that was stopping Bluey from achieving his potential was his equipment. During 1936 he got hold of one of Max Grosskreutz's machines and he taught himself about the qualities of this bike in comparison to other machines and as a consequence improved the speed of his own racers.

The West Ham supporters' club was now 14,277 strong and nationwide there were about 70,000 fans subscribing to like groups. It was said that many would turn out just to see the team's leathers on display and there was something to this. West Ham had its own cricket team, Bluey was opening batsman, and games between other speedway sides, West Ham Football Club and even Essex drew thousands of spectators. Once again West Ham were the bridesmaids in the League, finishing in third place and again reached the final of the London Cup, but this time they blew out to Harringay.

The England Test team at Belle Vue, 6 July 1935. From left to right: Alex Jackson (manager), Jack Parker (Harringay), Tommy Croombs (West Ham), Eric Langton (captain, Belle Vue), Tom Farndon (New Cross), Joe Abbot (Belle Vue), Bill Kitchen (Belle Vue); reserves Tiger Stevenson (West Ham), Bob Harrison (Belle Vue).

The Australian Test team at Belle Vue, 6 July 1935. From left to right: Dicky Case (Hackney Wick), Mick Murphy (reserve, Hackney Wick), Jack Sharpe (Wimbledon), Max Grosskreutz (Belle Vue), Vic Huxley (captain, Wimbledon), Lionel Van Praag (Wembley), Bluey Wilkinson (West Ham), Ron Johnson (New Cross).

Opposite: Jack Milne, USA.

Above: The 1935 Belle Vue team.

Opposite: Tommy Allott, Sheffield, 1938.

1935 National League

Team	PL	W	D	L	Pts
Belle Vue	24	18	2	4	38
Harringay	24	13	0	11	26
West Ham	24	12	1	11	25
Wembley	24	11	0	13	22
Hackney Wick	24	10	1	13	21
New Cross	24	10	0	14	20
Wimbledon	24	8	0	16	16

By the end of 1935, Belle Vue were acknowledged to be the world's finest speedway team. Proudly wearing their 'Ace of Clubs' tabards they had won the League Championship and National Cup in 1933 and 1934 and the ACU Cup in 1934. The 1935 League victory was the third in succession, and was accomplished despite the loss of the great Frank Charles. Five of Belle Vue's 1935 side had achieved Test recognition, including England skipper Eric Langton and one of Australia's most formidable riders, Max Grosskreutz. Other members of the team were Bill Kitchen, Eric Blain, Bob Harrison, Joe Abbot and Tommy Allott.

At Westhay Stan Dell, Ken Brett and Rol Stobart, all members of the junior side of 1934, were promoted to the senior team and along with Arthur Atkinson, Arthur

Ken Brett.

Warwick and Jack 'Broncho' Dixon, supported the West Ham top three, Wilkinson, Croombs and Stevenson.

Early in 1935 a £25, two-out-of-three challenge match race series was organized between Tom Farndon, the British Champion, and Bluey Wilkinson, the Australian Champion and the hottest challenger to Farndon for the national title. Tom ate up the big West Ham track, reaching speeds well over 45mph, smashing Vic Huxley's record of May 1934, beating Bluey in the process. However, the Speedway Control Board had not been consulted and forbade the match from taking the format of the official British Championship, as it would undermine the prestige of what was the premier speedway competition of the era. The board stipulated that the riders should meet for one race at West Ham and another at New Cross; there was to be no neutral decider.

The Star Riders Championship was radically altered in 1935. Tracks hosted qualifying rounds to produce a sixteen-rider final, which was fought out over 20 Wembley heats. All the finalists raced against each other once in four-man races (formerly the heats had been three-rider contests). The limitations of club representation relaxed, Wilkinson, Croombs and Stevenson were in the final. Stevenson finished in a disappointing equal eleventh. Croombs made ninth place, while Wilkinson finished equal fourth, but a shadow hung over that year's proceedings. The favourite for the title had been fatally injured in a crash at New Cross on the Wednesday before the final. It was the final of the Scratch Race, and the field included New Cross men Stan Greatrex, Ron Johnson and Tom Farndon, together with West Ham's Bluey Wilkinson. In the latter stages of the race Johnson struck the fence and fell. Farndon collided with his skipper's bike and was sent hurtling into the air. Johnson was not badly hurt but Tom was rushed to hospital in a critical condition. He died forty-eight hours later.

The Australian Test side was, once more, never without Wilkinson in 1935. Tommy was the top English scorer in the Custom House Test and was selected four times for the series. Tiger Stevenson, who had not had the best of seasons, appeared just once. Bluey made his usual trip home to Australia in 1935 and took the Australian Championship.

Maximum points, no cigar!

Bluey Wilkinson's performance in the 1936 World Championship final was and will always be exceptional. Not because he won, but because he scored maximum points and lost! No one else has ever repeated such a feat. Lionel Van Praag became the first ever World Champion but Wilkinson had won all five of his races on the night. Bluey was the victim of the bonus points system. Wilkinson qualified for the final with 10 bonus points, two less than Van Praag and three behind Eric Langton. In any post-war competition he would have been the World Champion. He scored a 15-point maximum but failed to become the Champion because he had scored fewer bonus points than Van Praag.

The prize money for that first event was £500 for first place, £250 for runner up and £100 for the third rider over the line – big money when one considers the average wage in 1936 was around £5. After the final there were some mumblings about Wilkinson being involved in a conspiracy with his countryman Lionel Van Praag to work together to organize results with the aim of accumulating maximum prize money. This gossip was resuscitated in the late 1990s by a fringe element of the speedway media along with other unsubstantiated allegations about Van Praag's victory over Langton. I have written elsewhere about this issue but for the purposes of this book it needs to be reiterated that there was no more ambitious or scrupulous rider in speedway than Bluey Wilkinson and given that he rode out maximum points it hardly seems likely that he was involved in any covert agreements. Even if he had been, that doesn't mean that other riders could not have come to similar types of accords with each other, which would of course have cancelled out the effects of other 'plots'. Anyway, such conjecture is something worse than a waste of time; in fact it borders on the malicious in relation to the surviving riders and all the families of the racers associated with that first World Championship.

Although hugely disappointed about the circumstances in which he was denied the inaugural world crown, 1936 did have some compensations for Bluey Wilkinson. Following a five-year courtship, he married Muriel at Caxton Hall. The ceremony was conducted by Muriel's uncle, the Chief Registrar of England no less. The couple had planned to marry after Bluey's retirement from racing, but because his career was booming and his potential earnings from speedway were likely to be relatively high for several more years, the marriage took place. It was a highly secretive and private celebration as Muriel and Bluey wanted to avoid the obligatory ride around the track at West Ham in Johnnie Hoskins' glass coach. Muriel's father had been interested in speedway from the beginnings of the sport and had business interests in bikes.

Bluey had been a favourite to win the World Championship and many of his fans were devastated by the way he lost. There were also a few that were very disappointed when he got married. At least one fan had felt so negative about the effects of marriage on his career she was moved to write:

9 10 1936

1 Path of Dreams
Heavens Highway
Paradise

Dear Bluey,

News-News-News and to think all about marriage with your photo in my locket. Now listen, think of the old saying, marriage is a lottery and also the downfall of all speedway riders as proved time and again so clear your head and don't let some fair lass cross your path with her hand out and also to ruin your career and cause many of your admirers to take gas.

Love, this thing called love you cannot let it take you to your grave far quicker than the cinders, and without you at the West Ham track the thrill has gone for us but you may think marriage is a thrill for you but it does not last as long as it has taken you Bluey dear to make a name for yourself and so cause me to have many a wonderful dream of you, and as I write this letter tears are falling from my big blue eyes. Oh how I hate to think of the girl that will take you from me so please Bluey darling consider your fate and seriously read these lines warning you of disaster.

How long must my suspense last and my love dreams shattered. Goodbye hope, how eagerly I wait further news.

From Your
Ever loving to a cinder

Brokenhearted Lover

All come and look for America

The advice of Brokenhearted Lover seemed not to deter Bluey and it is unlikely that he slept with it under his pillow while he and Muriel were on their honeymoon trip on the Queen Mary. Sailing over to America, Bluey and Muriel met up with Jack and Kate Milne and together they journeyed to Detroit where Jack's uncle had an automobile business. Bluey and Jack bought a car together and the two couples then set out to drive across America. This was not the last trip the group made. In all they traversed the United States together three times, 1936, 1937 and 1938. Muriel kept maps of their trips as a memento. Each year they chose a different route, but they would always start out in

The 1936 England Test team. From left to right: George Newton (New Cross), Bill Kitchen (Belle Vue), Jack Parker (Harringay), Eric Langton (captain, Belle Vue), Joe Abbot (Belle Vue), Harold Lees (reserve, Wembley), Frank Charles (Wembley), Gus Kuhn (reserve, Wimbledon).

Phil Bishop leads Roger Frogley.

Aub Lawson signs an autograph for a young fan outside Custom House Stadium.

Detroit and make for Kansas City where Kate's family lived. All the journeys concluded in Pasadena, Jack's home town, where Jack's brother would sell the car they had used. Bluey and Muriel loved travelling and sightseeing. Their journeys took in such places as the Salt Lakes in Utah, where others were attempting to break the land speed record on the hard, flat surface. Among their other destinations were the Painted Desert, Los Angeles and El Paso. The two couples were to remain friends and Muriel continued to correspond with Jack and Kate for more than half a century.

Bang at the Bottom

Bluey's experience in the World Championships seemed to be indicative of the Hammers' season. With Tommy Croombs and Tiger Stevenson out for long periods the side finished at the very foot of League table. Hoskins had chopped and changed the team around in search of results and brought in a number of new faces including Mick Murphy and Phil Bishop, who was to see out his racing career with West Ham. His recorded crashes number over 400 and there were probably many more. At the end of the 1936 season Phil broke a leg but Hoskins found some promising replacements including former electrician Eric Chitty from Toronto, Canada. In 1930 he had fought his way to second place in the Canadian Championship. For all 'Roarin' Johnnie's shuffling, West Ham's plummet to the basement of the League continued unabated. The side dropped like an overweight elephant wearing lead wellies and a cast-iron top hat, playing a steel piano pushed down the lift shaft of the Empire State Building.

1936 National League

Team	PL	W	D	L	Pts
Belle Vue	24	18	1	5	37
Wembley	24	15	0	9	30
Harringay	24	12	0	12	24
Hackney Wick	24	11	0	13	22
Wimbledon	24	11	0	13	22
New Cross	24	9	0	15	18
West Ham	24	7	1	16	15

1936 Provincial League

Team	PL	W	D	L	Pts
Southampton	16	10	0	6	20
Bristol	16	10	0	6	20
Nottingham	16	9	0	7	18
Liverpool	16	9	0	7	18
Plymouth	16	2	0	14	4

(Cardiff withdrew; results deleted.)

There had been little sign of the disaster to come at the start of the season. In fact, Bluey had won the pairs competition, the Coronation Gold Cup, with Arthur Atkinson as a partner. The duo hadn't set the preliminary rounds alight. At Harringay they couldn't afford to lose a single race and had to score maximum points in competition with the best racers in the world, but Bluey and Akko produced the goods.

Wilkinson was selected for the Australia Test side in all five matches of the series for the sixth consecutive season. This was an unprecedented and unique achievement in speedway. Up to the end of 1936 his career points total made him the third-best Australian rider in Test history. He also made the second-best Australian score in the series, equalling his 1935 achievement. The Custom House crowd that turned out for the Test match saw Hammers Arthur Atkinson and Tommy Croombs ride for England.

10

WILKINSON'S CHAMPS

West Ham started their League season at Custom House with local rivals Hackney Wick providing the competition. Hackney looked not a little disjointed. Morian Hansen was the only visitor to win a heat, but two firsts were the complete total for his efforts. Everything went just right for the Hammers and they romped home to a 57-25 victory with Wilkinson taking the most points (10). Arthur Atkinson wasn't far behind him (9) while Tiger Stevenson, Tommy Croombs and Broncho Dixon all played major supporting roles (scoring 8 points each). This was the start of a wonderful run of National Speedway League victories for West Ham. By the summer the Hammers looked nothing like the 'wooden spooners' of the previous term and by the start of October West Ham were champions following a 43-38 win over Belle Vue at Custom House. They led their nearest rivals Wembley, who had finished their League fixtures, by four points with a match in hand. The season had been a wonderful time at Custom House and this was evidenced by the membership of the supporters' club, which in the autumn of 1937 stood near to 40,000 people.

1937 National League

Team	PL	W	D	L	Pts
West Ham	24	18	0	6	36
Wembley	24	16	0	8	32
New Cross	24	16	0	8	32
Belle Vue	24	13	0	11	26
Hackney Wick	24	10	0	14	20
Harringay	24	9	0	15	18
Wimbledon	24	2	0	22	4

1937 Provincial League

Team	PL	W	D	L	Pts
Bristol	20	15	0	5	30
Southampton	20	13	0	7	26
Nottingham	20	11	0	9	22
Liverpool	20	8	0	12	16
Norwich	20	8	0	12	16
Birmingham	20	5	0	15	10

(Leicester withdrew: results deleted)

Keeping the Edge

In 1937 Hoskins organized one of many charity events he was to be responsible for at Custom House. This was attended by the Lord Mayor of London, Sir George Broadbridge, as the chairman of the National Hospital for Nervous Diseases. The event attracted some of the world's best riders including the new World Champion Jack Milne, former champ Lionel Van Praag and the star riders from Australia and England. Bluey and Milne had to race off for the trophy. It was a real struggle between the off-track friends. With knees and elbows flying about all the way, Bluey took the event. In races where bikes and skill were more or less even, the result often came down to the relative strength and stamina of the men involved. Bluey was always very fit. His endurance quality was borne of long days spent playing tennis in Australia; however, it had been in England where he had first worked with weights. Few sportsmen were doing this at the time, most basically relied on merely 'playing the game' and a few 'physical jerks'. Certainly hardly any speedway riders bothered with fitness routines as such in the 1930s. However, Bluey's star status meant that he mixed with other sportsmen, many of whom would attend Custom House on race nights, and being a listener and a learner, and a stickler for preparation, ready to try anything that gave him the slightest edge in competition, Bluey had developed a primal form of circuit training. Wanting to keep the means of his possible advantage secret, he kept very quiet about his training regime. Often using the Tottenham Hotspur football ground, White Hart Lane, as a venue, he ran and worked out behind closed doors, sometimes with coaches from the club and like the Powder Hall sprinters he made use of long sessions of speedball training. The strength and suppleness he developed would have certainly made a difference to his performance but the improvement that comes of such fitness in terms of speed of reactions would also have given Bluey that vital split-second timing that counts so much in speedway.

In 1937 Bluey was again a favourite for the World title, but at Belle Vue on the Saturday night before the first World Speedway Championships, Bluey was kind or careless enough to loan his best machine to a fellow racer. The rider crashed and Bluey's motor was badly damaged. At the next West Ham fixture at Wimbledon the track didn't suit his spare machine so he borrowed a bike from another competitor. Now it was his turn for a smack-up and he fractured a wrist bone (the only bone he ever

Above: Wembley Lions – League runners-up in 1937.

Right: 1937 programme.

Page 118: Joe Abbott.

Page 119: Wilbur 'Lammy' Lamoreaux.

Left: Eric Chitty of Canada.

broke) and twisted his already injured knee. As if this wasn't enough a sparkplug dug full depth into the muscle of his leg. The next night at West Ham he had to qualify for the World Championship. He was in terrible pain and had to be helped into the saddle. He raced, but with one hand. Even Bluey Wilkinson needed both hands when he was running against champions and he failed to qualify. At the World Championship Final, it was left to Eric Chitty, Tommy Croombs and Arthur Atkinson to carry the Hammers flag but Eric didn't have a great championship. Atkinson trailed him by a couple of places. Tommy Croombs propped up everyone else. Americans took first, second and third places. Wilkinson's great friend and rival, Jack Milne, won from Wilbur Lamoreaux and Jack's younger brother Cordy Milne took third place.

World Championship Final 1937

Pos.	Rider	Pts	Pos.	Rider	Pts
1	Jack Milne	28	11=	Morian Hansen	15
2	Wilbur Lamoreaux	25	11=	Eric Chitty	15
3	Cordy Milne	23	13=	Joe Abbott	14
4	Jack Parker	21	13=	Arthur Atkinson	14
5	Ginger Lees	19	15	Frank Varey	11
6=	Frank Charles	17	16	Tommy Croombs	2
6=	Lionel Van Praag	17		Alec Statham (Res)	0
8=	Bill Kitchen	16		Ron Johnson (Res)	DNR
8=	George Newton	16			
8=	Eric Langton	16			

There was only the one Test match in 1937 and of course Bluey was in the Aussie side and was top-scorer with 17 points. Arthur Atkinson brought home a dozen for the English. Atkinson was to get a couple more caps that year and Tommy Croombs rode once for his country. Eric Chitty was selected for the Overseas team three times; Bluey had to miss the first two of these matches due to injury. Charlie Spinks got a single ride in this series doing well to break into a wonderful array of international stars.

11

BLUEY WILKINSON WORLD CHAMPION

With Tiger Stevenson and Eric Chitty badly injured, West Ham could not hold on to the Championship, but finishing in second place to New Cross was no disgrace given the situation. Chitty, however, did become London Riders' Champion, the first West Ham rider to take the title. Bluey was easily top of the West Ham averages and his 10.63 gave him the third-best figures in the League. In the last nine West Ham fixtures he lost a miserly four points. Throughout the season he picked up enough material to start up in business as a silversmith. The flame-haired Aussie collected the Tom Stenner Cup, the *Daily Sketch* and the Knight of Speed trophies and the Tom Farndon Memorial Trophy.

England, as was becoming traditional, faced Wilkinson in all five Test matches. He top-scored in every one. With an 80-point total he created a new Test record that was to stand forever in the context of Australia *v.* England contests. In 38 Test appearances Bluey clocked up 359 points, almost 9.5 points in each match. But it was the World Championship that was to be Bluey's greatest victory and his glorious swansong. Wilkinson arrived at Wembley with the massive total of 53 qualifying points that converted to 8 bonus points. However, two other hot favourites had 7 points apiece; holder Jack Milne and Wilbur Lamoreaux. Eric Langton and Jack Parker also started out with a good cushion of points.

Injury crisis

Despite the news that some of the best qualifiers might not be able to compete, 93,000 fans were ensconced to watch the proceedings. A leg injury had made Lionel Van Praag doubtful, while Jack Milne had been struck down with the flu. However, Wilkinson was in dire straits. He had been making frequent trips to White Hart Lane for massage. His cartilage had been torturing him for weeks. He had a special knee harness made to relieve the stress, but had thrown it away after a somewhat limited period of experimentation. The little Aussie was ready to try anything, such was the pain, and he was persuaded by Johnnie Hoskins to give a psychic healer a try. Bluey had some belief in the concept of 'mind over matter' so decided to give Hoskins the benefit of the doubt and give it a whirl. The self-proclaimed 'ephemeralist' Reg Revins, an ardent West

West Ham 1938 – Bluey, flanked by Arthur Atkinson and Eric Chitty on his right and Tiger Stevenson and Tommy Croombs on his left, has the World Trophy in front of him.

Wilbur Lamoreaux, Australia, January 1948.

It's all academic – yet another trophy, presented by Professor Low.

Ham supporter, practised from a terraced house in Ilford. After getting Bluey to down a pint of Wyncarness fortified wine, he lit what looked like a large, cylindrical firework. It burnt quite placidly for a few seconds as Revins began to chant a sort of mantra, which sounded like 'Long, strong, black pudding' but then it started belching a glutinous, black smoke that quickly filled the room Bluey, Hoskins and Revins were occupying. Choking and coughing, they were forced to run from the house, but Reg, between splutterings, continued his dirge, 'Long, strong, black pudding'. Eyes streaming and lungs gasping for breath, patient, carer and healer staggered into the road outside Reg's palace of health restoration. Bluey limped away in anger and contempt, to the accompaniment of the fire-engine bells, the deep and noisy croup of Hoskins and Revins' intermittent elegy. That was Bluey's first and last dealing with alternative medicine. Wilkinson's troubles were multiplied when he was caught up in a serious crash in the final of a scratch race at New Cross the previous evening. Tom Farndon had been killed in the same event three years before. Bluey couldn't move his arm and was convinced that he broken his collarbone, but he spurned advice that he should have it X-rayed as it would mean he would not be allowed to compete in the World Championship final. On the morning of the final he made his way to White Hart Lane to undergo some intensive treatment from Tottenham Hotspur's physiotherapist.

Clem Mitchell and Len Stewart helped him there and the Aussie rider hung around to take him to Wembley, but Len had other urgent treatment to administer.

Wilkinson had been having some trouble with his machine at a meeting the Monday before the final. He and Len had taken it to pieces and rebuilt it. Wilkinson had tried the machine at West Ham on the Tuesday and was still unhappy. He took the bike to Custom House again on the Wednesday morning and raced with it on Wednesday night at New Cross where he crashed. While Bluey was attempting to get straightened out at Tottenham, Len stripped the motor down again and reassembled it for Bluey to ride on in the Thursday night World Championship final.

The Wembley Campaign

When Wilkinson got to the Empire Stadium he could hardly grasp the throttle. He was also incapable of getting his arm to shoulder level. Adding to his problems was an injury to his left leg; he literally had to be lifted on to the saddle of his machine each time he rode. Wilkinson was to spend the entire final swimming in a sea of pain.

If things looked grim then, they looked even more dire when Lamoreaux and Jack Milne strode into the pits. It seemed certain that the fates were against Wilkinson when he was drawn to ride against Milne in successive races, heats 4 and 5. He was also obliged to compete against the two favourites for the title, Van Praag and Lamoreaux, in the second of those heats.

Tommy Price, riding for Wembley Lions.

Tommy Price – preparation is all!

As the night wore on it became clear that this wasn't going to be the best World Championship ever. The riders seemed to be racing cautiously and it appeared that the first man out of the gate was winning the race without much of a challenge from those behind. Van Praag, Lamoreaux and Jack Milne all took maximum points from their initial races. Then it was Bluey's turn to ride, in heats 4 and 5. Bluey came out for the fourth heat wearing number 13. The three men he faced were all Belle Vue riders. Would they race as a team? Eric Langton was still as good as any man in the game. Frank Varey was not a lover of the Wembley track but the craggy but handsome Tyke was hard to beat. Another Northerner, Bill Kitchen, was also a tough and talented rider. Bluey was wearing a shoe instead of the regulation knee-boot. He'd had the shoe made for lightness and it was shod with gun metal. The reduced weight made him lighter overall but was also some relief for his injured leg. Bluey's first race started with the riders getting away as one, all vying to make the first turn. Bill Kitchen and Wilkinson wrangled for the initial fifty yards, but the Hammer got to the bend first and managed to hold off any challenge and win with some ease.

Before the next heat there was no time to think, apart from the moments it took to refuel. It was a daunting race. Bluey watched his foes line up: captain of Wembley Lionel Van Praag, the master of the Wembley dirt and a hot favourite with the stadium fans; the turbulent Yank Wilbur Lamoraux, the doyen of the Wimbledon supporters and never anything less than a difficult challenge and the inimitable and intimidating Tommy Price, like Van Praag a Wembley battler. Bluey had little doubt that the Wembley pair would, if given the chance, work together to hold the two outsiders back. Van

Praag wanted the title back and Bluey knew that this made Lionel the most dangerous of men. This was a 'must win' encounter if Van Praag was going to keep alive his hopes of bringing the Championship back to the Twin Towers. Within five minutes of winning heat 4, Bluey was back on the track and ready to start his next contest. Although leading from the start from the outside, Bluey was pressurized all the way by the Wembley captain, who rode one of the great races of his career to try and beat his fellow Australian. In the end Wilkinson come home a very clear winner. Heats 4 and 5 of the 1938 World Championships were remarkable performances given Bluey's condition. He won both contests in two of the fastest times of the final.

Wilkinson had some respite before having to come out again, but heat 12 came too quickly. Bluey faced his two fellow Hammers, Arthur Atkinson and Tommy Croombs. Both were out of the running and they surely would attempt to hold Bluey back. Alec Statham, the Harringay rider, made up the quartet. Statham was capable of riding brilliance but he was inconsistent and Bluey won at a relative canter.

Benny Kaufman, 'The New York Meteor', who rode for Southampton, was on the line looking at Bluey as the fourteenth race was about to begin. Benny was a bubbly, jovial type, and although lacking experience, Bluey's scalp would earn him some status, particularly among his fellow Americans. George Newton of New Cross, a marvellous fighter, who at times showed flashes of pure genius, pulled up to the line with Geoff Pymar of Wimbledon. Again, the quality of the field says much for Bluey, who took victory in his stride. George came from Ash Vale, near Aldershot, to the Crystal Palace training school at seventeen and, when hardly out of novice stage, equalled the West Ham track record. He rode with Tom Farndon in the New Cross

Bluey, Champion among Champions, West Ham, 1937.

George Newton.

team and modelled himself on the champion. He fulfilled his early promise in 1936, when he was top scorer for England in his first Test match. George shared second place in the World Championship preliminaries but a crash in the first heat cost him his chance in the final. The title was now within Bluey's grasp and everyone in the great stadium, that was then only fifteen years old, knew that with two more points to secure, the crown would be his. Heat 19 thus became the crucial race. Jack Milne, the Pasadena Panther, was waiting. As the 'Custom House Comet' moved up to the gate the ground were rousing for him. The race, the final, was now a conflict between the British Empire in the shape of Wilkinson and Jack Parker, and the USA represented by Jack and Cordy Milne. Jack had lost just one point all evening. He was just one point behind Wilkinson. If Jack had won and Bluey had followed him in, they would have had 14 points each. This would have been enough with Wilkinson's stash of 8 bonus points, one better than Milne's reserve. However, Jack Parker had to be considered and of course, Cordy Milne. The Californian Kid had won his second and third heats and Wilkinson could guarantee, given the opportunity, Cordy would hold him back. A win for Jack and Bluey in third would result in a run-off. Not for the first time Bluey felt the Yanks were out to get him!

This race was a contest of giants, each rider being a Champion in his own right. The knowledgeable Wembley crowd was tense with anticipation. The racers knew each other inside out and were among the best-known personalities in the sport. The roll round to the start seemed to take no time and a lifetime.

As the tapes leapt free, the first bike away on the outside of the track carried the Australian. His front wheel rode up and he was riding on his back tyre for a few dozen yards and there was some danger that he might tip backwards until he regained control, but he had been thrown out into the lead. However, Jack Milne was on terms at the first bend. Flouting the processional tradition of the evening, the elder of the brothers Milne moved with insight and intelligence and weaved his way to the front of the pack, coming out of the turn in the lead. Bluey hugged the line, with every intention of fighting out the next corner shoulder to shoulder, but as the huge Wembley track turned for a second time Wilkinson's powerful and practiced peripheral vision detected that Cordy and Parker were not a present threat to him and he was not about to take chances. Bluey began to position himself to stay several lengths behind Milne. But there was another race going on. Parker was fighting for the Empire and the former North American champion for family honour. Cordy understood that to deny Wilkinson was to elevate his brother and he wanted to be in the best position he could just in case Bluey slipped up. As such his tussle with Parker became an event in itself. Jack Milne hurtled home in first place and the next over the line was the West Ham rider. Bluey had done enough. His 22 points took the title. The section of the crowd from the crossed Hammers track celebrated. Claret and blue banners, hats and scarves lit up in the grand stadium.

Bluey rode sedately to the line and was presented with the cup. He said a few words on the loudspeakers to the vast crowd, thanking them. It was typical of Bluey that he also paid tribute to his mechanic and friend Len Stewart, saying that without his contribution he would not have managed to achieve his goal of winning the title at his third attempt, no one man being able to win the World Championship. Then he rode the sea of flashing lights that allowed the cameras to record his little bit of history. The cup, his trophy, glittered and winked in response. Wilkinson's injuries allowed him to be the only Champion not to be thrown in the air by the other competitors. The final had been the greatest test of his famous resolve and will. Wembley stood to acknowledge his remarkable achievement.

Ambitions fulfilled, dreams come true

Wilkinson was West Ham's first World Champion. Now he was more than a speedway star; he had, by winning the World Championship, become an international celebrity. In *The Times of Bathurst* (5 November 1938) it was reported that Bluey had:

> *…met and chatted with several of the talkie celebrities, among them being Lily Pond, Wallace Beery and Sonja Henie, the world- renowned Norwegian skater, and heroine in "A Girl in a Million" and other productions that captivated the talkie lovers the world over. Bluey found Sonja Henie charming company and a bright conversationalist. "She radiates joy and seemed a real happy-go-lucky girl" was how the speed ace expressed his impression of the Norwegian skater of grace and beauty.*

Wilkinson was now in high and consistent demand. There was hardly a racer that didn't want a crack at him and every promoter in Britain wanted an opportunity to demonstrate that their star rider or prodigy could match the Bathurst Blur. Bluey took on every pretender, racing, at times, at half-a-dozen meetings in a week. He was never to be defeated in a challenge match. Madame Tussaud's asked him to model for his likeness and he was the first speedway rider and one of the first sportsmen to be so honoured. The original intention was for Bluey to be depicted mounted on his motorcycle, head down, shoulders hunched, in the throes of competition. However, this would have made things a bit too complicated and full racing gear would have obscured his likeness. This being the case, Bluey's model was sat astride his motor, as if outside the pits waiting for the signal from the preliminary parade. Victor Martin made a gift of a brand-new machine (an early example of product placement) although Bluey corrupted the perfection. He always rode with the right handlebar set at such an angle so that his right arm was straight from the wrist to the shoulder when cornering. Bluey provided the riding gear. The distinctive blue scar below his left eye was also included. The figure survived the London Blitz and many thousands of Australians when visiting London made a pilgrimage to Bluey's model.

The winning of the World Championship was Bluey's goal from the time he saw his first speedway race. He had come back from the tremendous disappointments of 1933 and 1936 and won in what he knew to be his last chance. His knee injury would not allow another campaign. The silverware had indeed been flooding in. In his World title year Wilkinson also won the Tom Farndon Trophy at New Cross. For being top scorer in League racing he was awarded the Jessups Cup and for the best average score of the year he was awarded the Macready Cup. It is often forgotten that he won the Scottish Championship in Edinburgh in the same year and had been presented with his trophy by his mother who had travelled to Britain with her sister Jean. However Bluey's Aunt had to be back in Australia for the sheep-shearing season so they had to leave again in July. As such Bluey's mother wasn't able to witness her son's greatest triumph at Wembley.

1938 National League

Team	PL	W	D	L	Pts
New Cross	24	15	1	8	31
West Ham	24	13	1	10	27
Wembley	24	13	1	10	27
Wimbledon	24	12	3	9	27
Belle Vue	24	11	0	13	22
Harringay	24	10	1	13	21
Bristol	24	6	1	17	13

1938 programme.

Bluey Wilkinson, World Champion.

1938 Provincial League

Team	PL	W	D	L	Pts
Hackney Wick	16	12	0	4	24
Norwich	16	12	0	4	24
Southampton	16	9	0	7	18
West Ham II	16	8	2	6	18
Lea Bridge	16	8	0	8	16
Newcastle	16	7	1	8	15
Sheffield	16	6	1	9	13
Birmingham	16	6	0	10	12
Leeds	16	2	0	14	4

As was usual for Bluey and Muriel they went to Australia after the season. It was for quite a few months, particularly when he won the Australian Championship for a second and a third time. At the time the Australian Speedway Governing Body allowed up to three distinct Australian Solo Championships in one season over two, three and four laps at various tracks. Bluey won his three-lap and four-lap titles within three days of each other, one at the Sydney Showground and the other at the Sydney Sports Ground. Strange times.

12

OUT OF DARKNESS, LIGHT

In 1938, just after Bluey had won the World Championships, his wife Muriel gave a rare interview to Al Male of the Speedway Newsreel. In this piece it was said of the Wilkinsons that they were 'Two homely people, so natural that they don't realise how charming they are. That, of course is the secret of their popularity.' There always seems to be something behind the public lives of celebrities, but with Bluey and Muriel there just wasn't. They were a private couple but always deeply in love and totally committed to each other. Bluey liked to make home movies. He was an enthusiastic photographer, but the then new cine camera caught his imagination. On their trips across America, while visiting family in Bathurst, sightseeing either in England, America or Australia, Bluey would have his camera along with him and there are reels of film recording the wonderful places he and Muriel went to during the three short years of their marriage. In his family's photograph collection there's a snap of Bluey as a young boy dressed up as Ginger Meggs for a school occasion. Bluey was too reserved to think about becoming an actor but he was always interested in the theatre. Whilst in England it wasn't unusual for Muriel and Bluey to travel to Stratford-upon-Avon to take in some Shakespeare. They once took Johnnie Hoskins to see *Henry V* and had tremendous trouble quietening him down on the way back to London. The next match night Hoskins was reading quotes from the play over the Custom House sound system to the consternation and bewilderment of the Custom House supporters. My granddad told me that at least three supporters told him they didn't know it was a greyhound night and asked where they could get their money back!

Bluey was always last to arrive at tracks and always one of the first to leave. He hardly ever fraternized with the fans after meetings. He was invariably in a rush to get home to work on his racing machines or his car. He was a very fast driver but also careful and his driving licence carried no endorsements. Bluey seemed to be interested in everything. With his ability to listen and observe he could chat and debate on most issues and subjects. He regarded speedway as his job. When he left the track after a meeting he left his concerns and worries about the sport. At home, in their quiet flat with Muriel, he got on with the rest of his life. But even though this kind of behaviour, together with his natural shyness, led many to think that Bluey cared nothing for

At last – an all-British side! The Harringay team of 1935, from left to right: Charles Knott (promoter), riders Ron Mason, Norman Parker, Jack Parker (captain), Alec Statham, Dick Harris, Bill Pitcher, Les Wotton, Frank Dolan.

anybody and that his riding was no more than a business, a means to an end, wanting to win races and earn money, when West Ham lost he was as intensely disappointed as any supporter, other rider or the manager.

When the final year of the 1930s arrived it was by no means obvious that this would be the start of the most catastrophic period in world history. Early in the year, Bluey and Muriel were still in Australia. Bluey visited his family in Bathurst and raced at various meetings of the Australian season, but an old knee injury had begun to worry him. He failed to turn up at West Ham at the start of the season, but this wasn't a terrible worry for his manager as it was not unusual for Bluey to be away until Easter. Indeed Wilkinson was back in England before Good Friday and was once more racing. But the knee problem got no better. Bluey had had his share of falls but no one spill had caused serious injury, but it was becoming clear that the consequences of a decade of hard riding were now emerging. He was experiencing excruciating pain and as such, for his own safety and the good of others, including his family, he decided to retire from racing. 1938 had been Bluey's greatest year, the zenith of a brilliant career, and he finished at the very top. After his farewell ride he told the Custom House faithful how much he would miss them and the home of the Hammers. There were few totally dry eyes in West Ham Stadium as, for the last time in claret and blue, Bluey Wilkinson disappeared into the pits.

After Wilkinson had won the World crown, the press had asked him what he would do when he decided to finish racing. Without hesitation he replied that he would become a promoter just as his good friend Max Grosskreutz had done on retirement. Following the example of his compatriot, who was doing well as the manager of Norwich, Wilkinson did look to promotion and management for his future and took up a position with Sheffield, a concern that had recently gone into liquidation. He leased the stadium and on the opening night of the Steel City track he told the crowd that their team was going to beat any side in the land. Wilkinson managed Sheffield well and they showed signs of being able to challenge the more established teams. Bluey

Broncho Dixon, often a partner to Bluey.

required his riders to emulate his habit of thoroughness and diligence. All the riders had to tune their own machines and even the more experienced riders were required to change their ways under Bluey's regime. He began to draw in people he trusted and admired. For example, he brought Broncho Dixon in to help supervise the side's workshops. One of Bluey's main rivals for the Division Two championship was Newcastle who, for part of that season, would be managed by Johnnie Hoskins.

Without Wilkinson, and with Tiger Stevenson descending into a malaise of sluggishness, West Ham were destined to mediocre mid-table obscurity, but they did manage to avoid relegation under the new two-division system.

1939 National League (Div. 1)

Team	PL	W	D	L	Pts
Belle Vue	16	12	1	3	25
Wimbledon	18	12	0	6	24
Wembley	19	11	1	7	23
West Ham	19	9	0	10	18
Harringay	15	6	1	8	13
Southampton	17	5	0	12	10
New Cross	18	4	1	13	9

1939 National League (Div. 2)

Team	PL	W	D	L	Pts
Newcastle	15	10	0	5	20
Sheffield	9	8	0	1	16
Harringay	16	6	1	8	13
Norwich	12	6	0	6	12
Bristol	13	4	0	9	8
Belle Vue II	14	4	0	10	8

Top: The Lions of Wembley. From left to right: Alex Jackson (manager), George Wilks, Morian Hansen, Alex Menzies, Aub Lawson, Lionel Van Praag, Malcolm Craven, Tommy Price.

Above: Harringay Racers. From left to right: Mr Knott (managing director), R. Harris, W. Parker, L. Goffe, Jack Parker, S. White (masseur and trainer), Alexc Statham, Norman Parker, F. Dolan, L. Wotton, G. Kay (manager).

The Test series of 1939 was reduced to five matches, but only four were played due to the outbreak of the Second World War. The competition was resumed on 5 July 1947 with the first of three matches at Bradford. The crowd numbered 47,050.

Bluey's last ride

West Ham speedway had a history of VIP visitors under the reign of Johnnie Hoskins, including various members of 'the great and the good', the likes of the Lord Mayor of London. He even got Prince Philip, before he was the Duke of Edinburgh, riding a one-lap exhibition race as Phil 'the Greek Streak' Oldeburgh against Fred Pescarli, a friend of Hoskins who owned the dog meat stall in Rathbone Street market, Canning Town. Pescarli was an enthusiastic if totally inept amateur, who was a kind of occasional 'comic turn' at Custom House, although as far as he was concerned his involvement was deadly serious. Prince Philip, a Gordonstoun lad at the time, was at Custom House with his mother, Princess Alice of Battenburg, who, being congenitally deaf, something of an advantage in the West Ham pits, could lip read in several languages. Princess Alice was a great Hammers supporter, although her husband, Prince Andrew of Greece, never took to the sport, preferring the gaming tables of Monaco. Fred was also a great fan of the Hammers, following the team all over the country. Standing 5ft 1in tall in his stocking feet, it was rumoured Fred tipped the scales near the 18-stone mark. He was known to the fans as 'Verge' Pescarli, as he rode in grass-green leathers and pootled round the outside of the track so sedately that he hardly seemed to move at all. Fred claimed his dad had supplied dog food to Prince Philip's great-great grandma, Queen Victoria (also the great-great grandma of Prince Philip's future wife). But, he was no match for the horse-loving, boat-sailing Philip, who, accustomed to the saddle and swell, easily won the 'Pedigree Cup' that had been sponsored by Fred. But 'The Verge' had his fifteen minutes of fame, because that's how long it took him to get round the track. By the time he got over the line Princess Alice had presented her son with the trophy and was back in the stands tucking into a fish supper with him.

This of course, was an unofficial, informal visit but it wasn't long after that, on the evening of 6 June 1939, Hoskins managed to organize the first official Royal patronage of speedway when the Duchess of Kent attended a charity meeting at Custom House in support of a children's hospital. Viscountess Hinchinbroke (like Princess Alice, a regular visitor to Custom House) had helped arrange a Royal visit to the stadium for the event. Hoskins immediately advertised the evening's contests, including an appearance by Wilkinson. At this point Bluey knew nothing of the arrangements. Unfortunately the Viscountess arranged for the Duchess of Kent to turn up on the Tuesday following Bank Holiday Monday, a traditional greyhound racing day at Custom House. There was no question that the dogs could be cancelled so Hoskins was obliged to go back to his aristocratic contact and ask her to get the Duchess to shift her diary around. By now Hoskins had made sure the stadium had built a special Royal enclosure and box. The local council had already begun to bedeck the stadium with flowers and exotic trees.

Fortunately the Duchess managed to sort things out and a day was named. All that remained was for Hoskins to organise the appearance of the retired World Champion. The first two phone calls gave no more information than 'Bluey's not in'. The next half-

Ever-ready Aub.

a-dozen calls were unanswered. At this point Hoskins resorted to pleading in person and after some persuasion Wilkinson agreed to ride in a special match-race series against Arthur Atkinson, who had taken over as West Ham's number one. Atkinson was riding like a god at the time and was a hot favourite to win the next World Championship.

The Duchess didn't arrive until near the end of the evening, to be met by the band of the Welsh Guards and Josephine Croombs, eleven-year-old daughter of West Ham captain Tommy with a bouquet. The Royal occasion opened with a contest against Wembley. The visitors pummelled West Ham 36-48, ending a two-year unbeaten run at 'Fortress Custom House'. Then there was an 'International Championship' event that was made up of four heats and a final. The competitors for the latter spectacular, that included Tommy Croombs, Arthur Atkinson, Jimmy Gibb, Eric Chitty, Charlie Spinks, Colin Watson, Lionel Van Praag, Malcolm Craven, Aub Lawson, Bill Longley, Jack Milne, Jack Parker, Eric Langdon, Wilbur Lamoreaux and Cordy Milne, looked like a who's who of 1930s speedway greats.

The other big event was the race between the past and future champion. When the starting tapes hit the sky Bluey blasted into the lead. He rode like he'd never been away.

Chitty, the Custom House Cannonball.

On that evening Bluey would have defeated any rider. The gutsy Tyke Atkinson pursued the Aussie but was never going to catch him. Their second encounter on the night went the same way, making the potential third encounter redundant. Even though the Duchess asked Hoskins if they were to see more of the Champion, Wilkinson was never to ride again. Bluey had ridden magnificently. He had smashed the track record twice, as well as the one and two-lap rolling start times on a bike loaned from Paddy Mills, riding it only after having spent hours tuning it. Up to that race Arthur Atkinson's scores in the Speedway Cup competition were amazing. He commented after the race:

> *'The newspapermen all crowded round me afterwards wanting to know what happened. The only explanation I can give is that he beat me – and that was that. He went faster than I did. It was Bluey's sense of occasion. He could always pull out something a little bit extra.'*

Bluey was visibly moved when the Duchess presented him with his final speedway trophy on the track he knew so well. The evening had raised a huge £12,000 for charity.

Aub Lawson, West Ham
and Australia.

The night concluded with Cordy Milne winning the International Competition with his brother Jack making the runner-up position. He was followed home by Lamoreaux and Bill Longley.

However, there was a larger event which would overtake Duchesses, Champions and speedway. With the coming of the Second World War speedway was obliged to retreat. The World Championship final was scheduled for early September; it was never held. Britain's declaration of war on Germany happened a few days before the tapes were due to go up on the first heats at Wembley and all the sporting events were suspended. Bluey's track at Sheffield was closed and he got a job in a munitions factory for a while before he and Muriel returned to Australia and Bluey enlisted in the RAAF. Bluey, awaiting his call-up, had not been in New South Wales long when, in Sydney on 27 July 1940, he and Muriel were involved in a road accident. They were on their way home from the cinema; Bluey was driving a motorbike with Muriel as a passenger on the pillion seat. A truck swerved to miss an oncoming car and hit the couple. Bluey was killed instantly. So much disappeared so quickly.

Bluey – another winning ride
from the Bathurst Blur.

In his career Bluey was top-scorer for his own club in all League events every year from 1931 onwards. In Sydney he once had an unbroken sequence of thirty-eight wins. With Arthur Atkinson he won the Coronation Gold Cup for the best pair of riders in the country and he was awarded The Lord Mayor's Cup in 1937. He had won trophies at every speedway track of note in the United Kingdom and Australia. In the last racing year in addition to the World Championship and trophies won in Australia such as the Australian three and four-lap Championship and the NSW Championship he won the *Daily Sketch* Trophy at Wembley, the Scottish Championship at Edinburgh, the Tom Farndon Trophy at New Cross and at West Ham he practically swept the board, winning silverware including the Stratford Express Cup, the Knight of Speed Trophy, the May-Smith Cup, the Charles Boynton Cup, the Tiger Stevenson Cup and the Bridal Cup. He also won the Jessups Cup for being top scorer in the League and the Macready Cup for the rider with the best average score of the year. Many of Bluey's achievements would never be surpassed.

Muriel had been seriously injured in the crash that killed her husband. Because she was suffering bad head injuries, medical staff delayed giving her the news that Bluey

Bluey's ready – 1938 World Champion.

had died. The pain of the awful truth was added to when after she was told, Muriel was then informed that her husband had been already been buried.

The Western Times of Bathurst reported Bluey's funeral:

> *The funeral of A.G.(Bluey) Wilkinson, who was fatally injured when his motorcycle came into collision with a lorry on Old South Head Road, Rose Bay, on Saturday night, took place yesterday afternoon.*
>
> *The burial was made in the Church of England portion of the Bathurst cemetery. The funeral was probably the largest ever seen in Bathurst. It was attended by over 1,000 people, thus demonstrating the immense popularity of the World Champion speedway rider. Mr Frank Arthur, promoter of Empire Speedways Ltd, who was closely associated with Bluey during his brilliant career and Max Grosskreutz led the cortege in a car.*

The same newspaper reported that the Bathurst City Council had observed a brief period of silence at their last meeting as a mark of respect for a sportsman who had probably done more than any single person to put Bathurst on the map. Bluey's mother travelled to Sydney to support Muriel, who now found herself alone in a strange country and a widow. They became the best of friends and Muriel remained in Australia until after the war. In 1947 she returned to the United Kingdom with Max Grosskreutz and his wife. But Britain had changed and was almost as unfamiliar to her as Australia had been after Bluey's death. Muriel returned to Australia with the Grosskreutz's a year later. She spent the rest of her life in Queensland, only travelling back to England for short holidays.

Bathurst Remembers

Bathurst was never to forget Bluey Wilkinson. In 1947 Yeo & Mansell's, a local department store, put on an impressive exhibition of Bluey's trophies. It was a great success, with people coming from far and near to pay their respects. A similar display was organised in November 1989, in conjunction with a meeting to revive speedway racing in Bathurst and again was the source of tremendous interest. There is a street that bares Bluey's name in a suburb of Bathurst, in Windradyne. It is called Wilkinson Avenue, the same name as the road in Custom House that recalls his life and achievements. When the Bathurst District Sports and Recreation Council decided to put together a sports honour board, the first name nominated to be placed on the role of honour was Bluey's.

He was always proud of being Australian and particularly proud of his roots in Bathurst. As a World Champion sportsman, Bluey can be ranked with Bradman, Lindrum and Crawford as one of Australia's greatest sports stars. As I drove through New South Wales after visiting Bluey's birthplace and the city he loved so well, I couldn't help but contrast it to the place where he made his name and took the world, my home, the docklands where I was born and grew up. It is hard to imagine two more different places on a good day in New South Wales and a bad day in E16; heaven and hell almost. However, like Bluey, West Ham had given me a lot. It is a difficult place to live in and not the first area one might choose from which to achieve one's ambitions, to chase one's dreams. For all that, the place has a bubbling, boiling power; a tension that if you spend long enough looking out across the old docks into the Pool of London, as I did as a boy, you can smell and feel the awesome muscle of its history.

West Ham is an area soaked in the blood, sweat and tears of the working class. It was built on the terrible foundations of struggle, toil, hunger and early death. A hundred years before Bluey arrived, the shortage of labour saw men dragged from their houses and whipped into the docks. Not long before he was born, the dock workers were paid in tokens that could only be spent at dock shops. For many years the nutrition these dockets could be exchanged for amounted to not much more that 1,500 calories. This to feed men who were obliged to undertake the hardest of hard labour from before the first rays of light hit the murky waters of the Thames until the river was as dark as blistering pitch, burning up in excess of 5,000 calories a day. And families needed to be fed. This history has left a heritage of starvation from a legacy of industrial slavery. No wonder some of us seem to have been born angry! But this is where Bluey came, to bring excitement, passion and joy. As such it is so fitting that when new floodlights were

installed at the Bathurst Sports Ground in 1988, the site of the city's speedway until the start of the 1950s, the powerful illuminations were dedicated as a memorial to Wilkinson. Bluey shines on, making the darkest night bright. When the great lights of Custom House bathed West Ham stadium in whiteness and Bluey roared out to battle on our glimmering track with courage and defiance, he represented the hope that comes out of solidarity, the stuff our dreams are made of and what pulled East Enders through industrial oppression, war and social strife. It is the 'you wanna barney, then let's 'ave yer!' attitude which awaited the fascist leader Oswald Mosely and his black shirts as he tried to march into Canning Town at the time when Bluey was riding at his best. The racists thought more than twice when met by a wall of dockers and gas workers, Jews, gentiles and godless, armed with boathooks and solid steel boots. The same insolent belligerence greeted Hitler's bombers; the blitzkrieg that was supposed to bring us to our knees did just the opposite – in the words of Tom King, East London's bare-knuckle World Champion: 'I quit to no man!' That's why East London loved Bluey: we recognized one of our own; a proud fighter who didn't know when he was beaten and so never really lost.

Throughout the 1930s, his speedway decade, the little ginger geezer managed carburetion and captured the hearts of millions of people around the world, but particularly in East London and New South Wales. Perhaps that is his most fitting epitaph.

Opposite: Kangaroo Wilkinson at Belle Vue in 1938.

APPENDIX 1

SOME STATISTICS

West Ham with Bluey Wilkinson

1929-31 Southern League
1932-33 National League
1934 National League and Reserve League
1935-37 National League
1938-39 National League Division One.

League Champions: 1937
ACU Cup Winners: 1938

Bluey Wilkinson's Major Honours

1933	Third place in the Star Riders Championship
1934	New South Wales Championship
1935	Joint fourth place in the Star Riders Championship
1935	Australian Championship
1936	Third place in World Championship
1937	World Champion
1938	New South Wales Championship
1938	Australian Championship (3 Lap)
1938	Australian Championship (4 Lap)

Bluey Wilkinson's World Speedway Championship Record

1933 Star Riders Championship – Wembley

1st	Tom Farndon (England & Crystal Palace)
2nd	Ron Johnson (Australia & Crystal Palace)
3rd	Bluey Wilkinson (Australia & West Ham)

1936 World Championship Final – Wembley

1	Lionel Van Praag	26
2	Eric Langton	26
3	Bluey Wilkinson	25
4=	Cordy Milne	20
4=	Frank Charles	20
6=	Dick Case	17
6=	Jack Ormston	17
6=	Vic Huxley	17
9	George Newton	16
10=	Jack Milne	15
10=	Bob Harrison	15
10=	Morian Hansen	15
13	Wal Phillips	12
14	Ginger Lees	11
15	Arthur Atkinson	9
16	Bill Pitcher	8
	Norman Parker (Res.)	7
	Balzer Hansen (Res.)	DNR

Opposite: 'Wee' Georgie Newton of New Cross and England, 1938.

Right: Wal Phillips.

Norman Parker, Wimbledon.

1938 World Championship Final (Wembley)

Score Chart

Pos.	Rider	Country	1st race	2nd race	3rd race	4th race	5th race	Total	Bonus	Grand Total
1	Bluey Wilkinson	Australia	3	3	3	3	2	14	8	22
2	Jack Milne	USA	3	3	2	3	3	14	7	21
3	Wilbur Lamoreaux	USA	3	1	3	3	3	13	7	20
4	Lionel Van Praag	Australia	3	2	2	1	3	11	7	18
5=	Bill Kitchen	England	2	2	1	2	2	9	6	15
5=	Cordy Milne	USA	1	3	3	0	1	8	7	15
7=	Alec Statham	England	2	3	0	0	3	8	5	13
7=	Eric Langton	England	1	2	2	3	0	8	5	13
9	Benny Kaufman	USA	2	1	0	2	2	7	5	12
10=	Jack Parker	England	2	2	2	0	0	6	4	10
10=	Arthur Atkinson	England	1	0	2	1	1	5	5	10
12=	Tommy Price	England	1	0	1	2	0	4	4	8
12=	Tommy Croombs	England	0	1	1	1	1	4	4	8
14=	Geoff Pymar	England	0	0	1	0	1	2	5	7
14=	George Newton	England	0	1	0	1	0	2	5	7
16	Frank Varey	England	0	0	0	ns	ns	0	4	4
	Jack Ormstom (res)	England				3	2	5	–	–
	Jimmy Gibb (res)	Canada	Did not ride							

Left: A man for all seasons, Alec Statham. *Right:* Benny Kaufman, USA.

1938 World Championship Final (Wembley)

Heat by Heat

Heat	Riders	Time (secs)
1	Van Praag, Parker, Atkinson, Pymar	76.8
2	Lamoreaux, Stratham, C. Milne, Newton	75.0
3	J Milne, Kaufman, Price, Croombs	77.4
4	Wilkinson, Kitchen, Langton, Varey	76.0
5	Wilkinson, Van Praag, Lamoreaux, Price,	76.2
6	C. Milne, Langton, Croombs, Pymar	77.8
7	Stratham , Parker, Kaufman,Varey	76.0
8	J. Milne, Kitchen, Newton, Atkinson	77.0
9	C. Milne, Van Praag, Kitchen, Kaufman,	77.2
10	Lamoreaux, J. Milne, Pymar, Varey	76.6
11	J. Milne, Langton, Van Praag, Stratham	75.8
12	Wilkinson, Atkinson, Croombs, Stratham,	78.0
13	Langton, Parker, Price, Newton	77.6
14	Wilkinson, Kaufman, Newton, Pymar	77.4
15	Lamoreaux , Kitchen, Croombs, Parker	76.0
16	Ormston, Price, Atkinson, C. Milne	77.6
17	Van Praag, Ormston, Croombs, Newton	78.2
18	Stratham, Kitchen, Pymar, Price,	76.8
19	J. Milne, Wilkinson, C. Milne, Parker	77.4
20	Lamoreaux, Kaufman, Atkinson, Langton	77.6

APPENDIX 2

THE POETRY OF RATIO

To check or change the compression ratio, you require a 50cc burette and water, as this will not penetrate past the piston rings if the barrel and piston are well smeared with oil during assembly and the surplus wiped off before fitting the head. Lean the engine over until the plug hole is level and allow the water to fill the combustion space up to the bottom of the plug hole. This amount (say 35cc) is then added to the swept volume of the piston (497cc + 35cc = 532cc), which total is divided by the measured amount (35), giving in this example a compression ratio of 15.2:1. Compression plates are available in three thicknesses – $\frac{1}{64}$in, $\frac{1}{32}$in and $\frac{1}{16}$in. The $\frac{1}{64}$in plate will increase the combustion space by 2cc. This knowledge will save remeasuring if the original assembly needs to be modified. Turn the engine upside down to drain the water out. If the head is not to be removed again, a little methanol fuel can be introduced into the head; this will help to disperse the water and prevent rust. Empty the methanol out and turn the engine a few times to allow the remaining fluid to evaporate. This adjustment would not be carried out at a meeting or between races but in the workshop before setting out for the track.

Gear Ratio Chart

Most riders carried this with them; the gearing was often adjusted up or down during the meeting to suit the track conditions.

Rear sprocket	Clutch	Engine	Crank-shaft	Gear ratio
58	44	20	17	7.5
58	44	19	17	7.6
58	44	20	16	7.9
58	44	19	17	7.9
57	44	20	15	8.36
58	44	19	16	8.4
60	44	21	15	8.4
59	44	18	17	8.48
57	44	21	14	8.5
58	44	20	15	8.5

INDEX

If you are interested in purchasing
other books published by Tempus, or in case you have
difficulty finding any Tempus books in your local bookshop,
you can also place orders directly through our website

www.tempus-publishing.com